Images *of the* Dove

Images *of the* Dove

Jean Hansell

Millstream Books

for Peter
who also loved the birds

ROCK DOVE.

First published in 2003 by
Millstream Books, 18 The Tyning, Bath BA2 6AL

Set in Palatino and printed in Great Britain by
The Amadeus Press, Cleckheaton, West Yorkshire

© text Jean Hansell 2003

ISBN 0 948975 68 7

British Library Cataloguing-in-Publication Data:
a catalogue record for this book is available from the British Library

CONTENTS

Detail from a stained-glass window by Frank Brangwyn (see page 160).

The endpapers were painted by Barbara Frears from a photograph by David Hansell of an altar frontal in the church of Santo Spirito in Florence.

ACKNOWLEDGMENTS

After completing *The Pigeon in History* five years ago, it became apparent that not only could the story be usefully expanded but that there was also a wealth of related artistic material produced over many centuries which ought be published. This book is the result of my endeavours but it would not have been possible without the help and encouragement of many people to all of whom I am extremely grateful.

Firstly, I am greatly indebted to artist and friend Barbara Frears whose drawings and watercolours have been of inestimable value in enlivening the text of this book and all three previous ones on the subject. She has also been a great help in advising about matters of layout and other aspects of publication.

Thanks are also due to members of my immediate family who have contributed illustrations to the book and have always been on the lookout for relevant material in their travels both at home and abroad. To my son David I am particularly indebted for help with transcribing the final manuscript and vetting the finished book. I am grateful also to Ann Gaskell-Taylor and to Patrick Gaskell-Taylor who have supplied me with a regular succession of cuttings from the printed press, and to Neil and Leila Wishart for proof-reading. Thanks are also due to Dr Daniel Haag-Wackernagel of Basel and Dr Irit Ziffer of Tel-Aviv, whose books on the subject of doves have both informed and inspired me.

I am grateful to countless individuals and employees of galleries, museums and libraries around the world for their help in supplying references and illustrative material. The staff of the Bodleian and British Libraries, and particularly the latter's Department of Manuscripts, have invariably proved most helpful in response to my innumerable requests for information.

Illustrations in the book have been credited appropriately where possible. Some material, however, has been supplied to me without full provenance and to the owners of any material which I have been unable to credit successfully I beg indulgence.

My appreciation, as always, to Tim Graham of Millstream Books who took on this book, his fourth on the subject, and has maintained his exemplary attention to detail throughout the publishing process. He has been a pleasure to work with and has also been a great support at all times. In this connection I would like to mention the number of other publishers who, over the years, have congratulated me on the concept of this book but who have failed to realise the idea.

Finally there is my gratitude to my late husband Peter, who not only gave me immeasurable help and encouragement during the early stages in the preparation of the book, but also transcribed my original manuscript and at all times helped me with various technical aspects, particularly those concerned with photography.

PROLOGUE

> All art is both surface and symbol, those who
> look below the surface do so at their peril.

In the world of art, Oscar Wilde's dictum could well apply to the dove. Among the many images to be found in art the dove must count as one of the most beautiful and intriguing. In ancient times birds were revered and worshipped as spiritual links between heaven and earth, the dove, in particular, being coupled with the great mother goddess whose symbol of fecundity it became. In tracing the history of the bird through the ages there is abundant evidence of its endurance in iconography, even until the present day.

Earlier images range from the crude terracotta figures of the Near East and Eastern Mediterranean, dating from the third millennium B.C., to the later legends of Aphrodite (Venus) and her dove in the form of coins, bronzes, statuary, bas-reliefs, cylinder seals and lamps, as well as frescoes, mosaics and vase paintings.

At the beginning of the first millennium the Old Testament story of Noah and the dove was incorporated in early Christian funerary monuments and wall paintings in the Roman catacombs. In the New Testament, the baptism of Christ, in which the dove descended as the holy spirit, was also an early subject in Christian art, because baptism and the eucharist were the two original sacraments of the church. From the 12th century onwards, as artistic techniques developed, the dove appeared in illuminated manuscripts, stained glass, woodcuts, engravings and paintings. The later interpretations of the Renaissance, with its renewed interest in the classical world, lent new meaning and inspiration to the dove symbol in many great works of art.

The perpetuation of the dove image through the ages has reflected not only its early historical significance, but also the bird's close and unique relationship with man. This affinity is nowadays less appreciated than in the past. Nevertheless, no other bird has had such close links with man, nor been useful to him in so many ways. It has served him as symbol, sacrifice, source of food and, not least, as messenger both sacred and secular. It is no ordinary bird.

The complete story of this remarkable bird has been much obscured by the age-long confusion between the terms 'pigeon' and 'dove', both of which are still in use today. In general 'dove' is traditionally reserved for use in the aesthetic contexts of religion, literature and art and 'pigeon' for more mundane matters such as sport, fancy breeds and culinary use. It is not immediately obvious that the Old Testament dove of Noah and the New Testament dove of the Holy Spirit were ancestors of the dovecote birds of the more recent past or the multitudes of urban pigeons found all over the world today. Nor does

7

there seem to be an obvious resemblance between the white dove of peace and the pigeon in a pie, but all these birds are directly descended from the wild Blue Rock Pigeon (*Columba livia*).

The white dove is a familiar symbol nowadays. In this age of consumerism it features widely on greeting cards of all kinds and is even incorporated in advertisements and wine labels, and in one notable example a dove appears as a hologram on a well-known credit card. The image of the dove carrying an olive branch, which dates back to the story of the dove returning to Noah in the ark, has become an international symbol of peace and reconciliation. The political adage 'hawks and doves' is often cited nowadays, for example during the events preceding the recent conflict in the Middle East. Peace marches in many parts of the world, with participants often carrying dove banners, led to some media reports naming the occasion 'The Day of the Dove'. Early in 2003, at a meeting of members of the European Union in Athens to celebrate the accession of ten new members, a group photograph at the foot of the Acropolis showed members posing for the camera each wearing a white dove lapel-pin given to them by the President of Greece, while many of those in the front row held an olive branch in their hands. A model of a giant white dove dominated the scene.

The dove continues to be a popular emblem of peace and goodwill and a source of inspiration in art even though much of its earlier symbolism is now forgotten. Sadly it cannot be said that its cousin, the urban pigeon, is a very popular bird nowadays. In the cities of the world where most of them now live they are much in the public eye but are generally regarded as a civic nuisance. The result is that in many cities people are divided into those who love the bird and those who detest them as 'flying rats'. Sadly, this current prejudice overlooks many aspects of the birds long history and fails to acknowledge the great debt owed to it in the past; it is not just any other bird.

Man's association with the dove has not always been to the bird's benefit. It played a minor role as bait and decoy in the sport of falconry and was massacred by the hundred in the English pigeon-shooting matches of the 19th century. Today, however, the gentler pursuits of pigeon-racing and fancying have a large following in many parts of the world. In such activities, the strong bond of affection that often exists between owner and bird is an aspect which is not widely recognised.

In fact, the birds have had so many different roles, as symbols of gods and goddesses, sacrificial victims, messengers, pets, food and sometimes more than one of these at the same time, that one cannot help thinking that we've put too much on them. To love them for their homing instinct and then to use that instinct for sport or war might seem like exploitation. But the present prejudice that exists against the city pigeons is probably the greatest irony of all. Our past debt to the bird should not be forgotten.

EARLY IMAGES

Sumerians in Mesopotamia, modern Iraq, were the first to breed the white dove from the native Blue or Common Rock Pigeon (*Columba livia*), though exactly when this happened, and whether accidentally or by design, is unknown. Centuries later, Charles Darwin convincingly established that the wild pigeon was the common progenitor of the innumerable varieties of fancy pigeon which can be produced by selective breeding. A clue to the chance emergence, in the past, of the white variation lies in the white rump which often features in the wild bird. To ancient people the appearance of the white pigeon must have seemed miraculous and would account for the sacred role it held in early years.

The early days of dove/pigeon worship date back to a time when primitive man worshipped the all-powerful Mother Goddess, with whom the bird was inextricably linked and whose symbol of fertility it became. The bond between them stemmed partly from the bird's exceptional fecundity, two eggs being laid eight times or more each year in southern climes. Apart from this biological quirk, the bird was also regarded, together with other birds flying out of the distant sky, as a messenger of wonder and a visible incarnation of the invisible world. Together with the eagle it was one of the most elemental sky-heaven symbols but it stressed purity and innocence rather than power and it was therefore also the opposite of the serpent emblem. In very early days the dove was used on Assyrian banners to denote truth and innocence which was later adopted on a Christian banner depicting the Holy Ghost.

The Mother Goddess, who was believed to be immortal, changeless and omnipotent, was thought by early man to possess the power of life, death and regeneration of plants and animals, as well as humans. As goddess of the sky, earth and waters, her symbols included the bird, serpent and fish, while the egg and womb were used to signify her procreative influence. The moon was also an important image, due to the association of its monthly waxing and waning with the fertility of women; its cyclical phases also being interpreted as the resurgence of new life after death.

The archaeological discovery of lifelike dove images, sometimes alongside figures of the goddess and dating from the Bronze Age (2400-1200 BC) and earlier in Mesopotamia, Crete, Cyprus, Iran and Greece, confirms these ancient roots. Most of these early figures of the bird are made from clay or terracotta, some being crudely fashioned, but others are more realistic and carry coloured decoration.

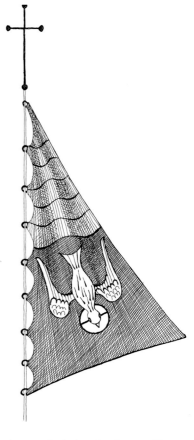

Banner depicting the dove emblem. (Barbara Frears, from Adolphe Didron, Christian Iconography, *1851)*

Painted terracotta images of doves from Cyprus, c.700 BC. (British Museum, painting by Barbara Frears from a photograph by Peter Hansell)

9

(above left) Egyptian figure of a dove in dark brown glass, 1000-700 BC. (Irit Ziffer)
(above right) Votive dove in lapis-lazuli with gold studs, from the Acropolis of Susa, Iran, c.1150 BC. (Louvre, Paris, France/Bridgeman Art Library)
(below left) Glass lamp of Byzantine origin, with a dove image on the stopper. (Irit Ziffer)
(below right) A pair of 'billing' doves carved in stone, from Mesopotamia, 2900-2800 BC. (Irit Ziffer)

Among the many images exhibited at the Eretz Israel Museum in Tel Aviv are some of exceptional interest, including glass figures, one of which has white thread decoration, and a rare lapis-lazuli model with inlaid gold studs from Iran. A pair of facing doves carved in stone, which comes from Mesopotamia and dates from 2900-2800 BC, is a less common theme and may be a forerunner of the facing dove symbol of later centuries. This is one of the earliest examples of the characteristic mating behaviour of the birds called 'billing', later described by Aristotle and aptly summarised by Bartholomew the Englishman in the 13th century: 'they kiss or bill each other before the treading'.

The recent find at Vukovar, Croatia, of a well-preserved dove model, claimed to date from the same period, must count as one of the earliest examples in Eastern Europe. It is described as a terracotta cult vessel and is embellished with linear encrusted decoration. The bird has a peak at the back of its rather flattened head.

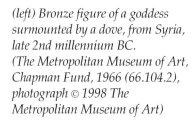

The Vukovar Hen Pigeon from Croatia, possibly dating from 2900-2800 BC. (Josip Pekanovic)

Some of the earliest depictions of the goddess together with her doves in the Near East date from the 18th to the 14th century BC. The birds are shown on stone moulds or clay plaques, either perched on her shoulders or on her throne, while others are held in her hands. More rarely they are seen perched on her head as in the Syrian figure fashioned in bronze, which dates from the 2nd millennium BC. Over the centuries the innate tendency of tame pigeons to perch on the heads or shoulders of those who feed them can still be

witnessed among feral city birds today. Some early cylinder seals depict the goddess, occasionally winged and accompanied by her dove, and holding what appears to be a mirror in each hand. Much later, the back of an Etruscan mirror shows the Greek goddess Leda with her swan, together with the dove of the goddess Astarte who holds a mirror in one hand. Do these early mirror symbols of the goddess foreshadow the astronomical mirror emblem associated with the planet Venus which, centuries later, was sometimes carried by the figure of Prudence? Very occasionally a male god is linked with the bird.

(left) Bronze figure of a goddess surmounted by a dove, from Syria, late 2nd millennium BC. (The Metropolitan Museum of Art, Chapman Fund, 1966 (66.104.2), photograph © 1998 The Metropolitan Museum of Art)

(below) Shrine model with doves and snakes from Beth Shan, 11th century BC. (Barbara Frears, from A.O. Cook, Zeus, God of the Bright Sky, *1914)*

The serpent was linked with the goddess in very earliest times. It was believed to symbolise the creative source and the life of the earth and also represented the image of her son and consort who died and was born again from her in an unending cycle. A rare and early representation of the dove and serpent together was found on an engraved golden goblet from Afghanistan dating from 3000 BC. These two symbols are also splendidly shown on early Assyrian clay shrines and later on models excavated from the 11th-century BC Canaanite temples of Beth Shan.

غلا ما رفق بجنان سبے فی الطریق نینے یدیہ اد جلس الغلام ریبول بے اصل حایط خرج حیہ صغیرہ یا

(above) Miniature from the arabic translation of Galen's Book of Antidotes, *showing a boy bitten by a snake. Note the haloed dove with other haloed birds in the trees.*

(below) Roman coin showing a sacred stone and fish with facing doves on either side. (Barbara Frears, from Eugène Goblet, Count d'Alviella, The Migration of Symbols, *1894)*

In the Near East the Tree of Life was believed to unite Heaven and Earth and was thought of as the primary image of the goddess herself, while the serpent was regarded as its guardian. Her son-lover was also closely linked with the Tree and together they symbolised the cyclical nature of life and death. Early Sumerian seals depict the goddess with the Tree of Life and serpent and occasionally a dove symbol is included. The two are graphically linked in a miniature from the arabic translation of Galen's *Book of Antidotes* written c.1250 AD. The scene depicts a boy bitten by a snake attempting to cure himself by killing and eating the reptile while a male figure, possibly a physician, looks on. The inclusion of a haloed dove in flight together with several haloed birds in the tree alongside suggests a Christian overlay with an allegorical interpretation of good (the pigeon) versus evil (the serpent). The fish was also regarded as a symbol of fertility and rebirth and being a silent inhabitant of the deep was perceived to be divine and sacred. The worship of fish and pigeon was recorded by Xenophon at Hierapolis in Anatolia in the 5th century BC, but was common elsewhere in the Near East. A stamp seal from Nippur in Mesopotamia, dating from this era, shows two facing pigeons on either side of a fish, while a later Roman coin shows facing doves standing on a cone above a fish. A silver coin showing the dove alone as the emblem of the city of Ashqelon was minted there in the 2nd century BC and centuries later a similar motif was perpetuated on a Roman coin from Mesopotamia.

The ancient Sumerian goddess Ishtar, one of several descendants of the Mother Goddess, symbolised Mother Earth in the natural cycles of fertility on earth. She was also the goddess of love and her most important rite involved ritual prostitution in the cult dedicated to her. Temples to her were inhabited by priestesses and prostitutes who enacted a sacred marriage symbolising Ishtar and her consort Tammuz to ensure a good harvest in the forthcoming year. In the legends, she went in search of him in the Underworld and finally restored him to life again. It has been postulated that the dove's natural affinity with man, allied to its tendency to nest in his dwellings, would have encouraged its domestication in such temples of the early goddesses where it would have been available for ritual sacrifice. The discovery at Al Ubaid, near Ur, Abraham's native city in southern Mesopotamia, of the remains of the temple to the goddess Ninhursag, who was called Queen of Heaven and Earth, which dates from 3000 BC, provides one of the earliest pieces of evidence for this conjecture. On the reconstructed outer façade, one of several limestone friezes shows a row of sitting pigeons. The birds are seen in a squatting position, which is true to life.

Links between the goddess and her doves and snakes were found in Crete during excavations by Arthur Evans early last century. A colourful group of figures dating from c.1500 BC found in the palace at Knossos included the clay image of a goddess with upraised hands and a dove on her head, whom he called 'Lady of the Dove'. In addition to other figures with doves were three painted fetish columns topped with birds; an unusual terracotta group of a lyre player and dancers around a dove; and several elegant snake-goddesses. Excavations by Heinrich Schliemann in the 19th century of royal tombs at Mycenae in southern Greece have revealed many treasures of gold, silver and faience made by craftsmen who may have been influenced by Cretan culture.

A silver coin minted at Ashqelon in the 2nd century BC, showing the dove as emblem of the city. (Irit Ziffer)

(left) Doves on the reconstructed façade of the temple to Ninhursag at Al Ubaid, c. 3000 BC. (British Museum, photograph by Peter Hansell)

Cretan dove-goddess from the palace of Knossos, Crete, c.1500 BC. (Barbara Frears, from Arthur Evans, 'The Palace of Knossos', in The Annual of the British School at Athens, No.VIII, *1902)*

Ornaments of gold-foil repoussé work from Mycenae, c.1500 BC. (National Archaeological Museum, Athens)

Several beautifully preserved, small ornaments of gold-foil *repoussé* work, also dating from around 1500 BC, and possibly associated with a sepulchral cult, were found there. One of these depicts the goddess with three doves in flight around her, while another represents a shrine or altar on which a pair of birds is perched.

In Cyprus, the discovery of innumerable terracotta bowls and cups, many of which are decorated with figures of doves, suggest that the birds may have been bred on the island as early as the 3rd and 4th millennia BC. Images of the dove as votive or sacrificial offerings, either alone or carried by postulants, or as the deities themselves, have also been found. Early figures of two women worshippers carrying doves, dating from 750-600 BC are crudely executed, but a later example of the goddess Artemis (Diana) with head-dress is much more ornate, as is the well-known limestone figure, 'The Priest with the Dove'.

Two small terracotta shrines from Transjordan, dating from 1000-800 BC, each carry a dove with outstretched wings above the main entrance. This may indicate the deity to whom the shrine was dedicated. A variation of the theme is found in the clay model dovecotes of Cyprus, two of which have rows of flight-holes in the upper walls and a bird-woman creature looking out of the shrine.

(above left) Marble doves from Mycenae. (National Archaeological Museum, Athens)

(above) The goddess Artemis carrying a dove, from Cyprus. (Barbara Frears)

(left) Clay model of a shrine, from Transjordan, c.1000 BC. A dove with outstretched wings looks out above the architrave; the double volute capitals are believed to represent the Tree of Life. (Collection of the Israel Antiquities Authority, photograph by Leonid Padrul)

15

CLASSICAL ART

The image of the Great Mother Goddess as supreme deity was deeply ingrained in ancient Greece, as in many other early cultures of the Near East and eastern Mediterranean. The Greek goddess Aphrodite, who became the Roman Venus, with her dove symbol was a successor of the early Mesopotamian, Assyrian and Phoenician goddesses, such as Semiramis, Ishtar and Astarte. When Zeus (Jupiter) became ruler of the gods and mortals, also chief sky-god and solar deity, Venus was relegated to a relatively minor role in the Pantheon. Although her ancestry was concerned with profound issues of life and death, later referred to by Plutarch in the first century as "presiding over birth and

death", she appears to have been known by the Greeks as goddess of love in both its sensuous and chaste forms and was also believed to epitomise beauty and grace both in herself and in nature. She retained her dove symbol, but it seems to have been shared with other deities. For example, Athene (Minerva),

goddess of wisdom and war, attributes formerly attached to the early Mother Goddess, is sometimes seen holding a dove; Demeter (Ceres), the corn goddess, who shared not only the dove symbol, but also the snake; and Artemis (Diana) who, in her pre-Greek origins, was a moon-goddess and was sometimes portrayed with a dove. A lesser figure in Greek and Roman mythology and widely represented in both Hellenistic art and in the later Renaissance was Eros (Cupid or Amor). His presence in art is usually symbolic and he features as a reminder that the particular theme is about love. Probably worshipped in the beginning as an early son-lover of the goddess, his importance gradually waned. At first he became subordinate to Aphrodite as an instigator of sexual love, but finally he played the part of a wayward winged youth who

Eros (Cupid) riding on a dove handle of a pottery vessel from Cuma, central Italy, c.320 BC. (British Museum, photographs by Peter Hansell)

shot arrows of infatuation and desire at random into his victims. Several illustrations capture his mischievous character and confirm his enduring link with Aphrodite and her dove. The story of the love between the god of war Ares (Mars) and Aphrodite and their discovery by Hephaestus (Vulcan) was a familiar one in classical mythology. In Roman times the dove symbol of Venus and the helmet emblem of Mars shown separately enthroned was a way of representing these deities. In the Renaissance the combined emblems were sometimes featured together as shown in a 16th-century manuscript which depicts Venus, her chariot drawn by doves, with helmeted soldiers in the foreground (see page 111).

The conception of the soul-bird or psychopomp, meaning the bearer of souls to the next world was a familiar belief in antiquity. Birds with powerful wings, such as eagles, were regarded as suitable for the role and able to make the journey heavenwards. They were sometimes portrayed in this way in Roman funerary art, while in Christianity the function was often assumed by angels. The Greek god Hermes (Mercury) was sometimes known as Hermes Psychopompus because he accompanied the souls of the dead to the Kingdom of Hades. His winged feet and vestigial wings would hardly have fitted him for the skyward journey. In early Egyptian art the soul-bird sometimes had a human head, which, in a modern reproduction, is given the body of a falcon (see next page). Early literary evidence for the dove as soul-bird in Judaism and Christianity dates from the 3rd to 4th centuries AD in the writings of St Ambrose: "That soul is blessed, simple in every respect. That soul is accordingly a dove."

17

A winged Egyptian soul-bird visiting a corpse. (British Museum, photograph by Peter Hansell)

THE SOUL OF THE SCRIBE ANI IN THE FORM OF A HUMAN-HEADED HAWK REVISITING HIS BODY IN THE TOMB

Zeus himself also appropriated the dove symbol, chiefly in connection with his oracular role. The earliest such shrines in Greece were dedicated to the woodland goddess, Dione, known as the triple goddess of the dove and oak cult and legendary mother of Aphrodite. The famous oracle at Dodona endured for centuries and Greek coins depict doves perching on trees, sometimes on either side of Zeus himself.

Although many early images of Aphrodite have been lost over the centuries, Geoffrey Grigson, writing some 20 years ago, estimated that more than 2,000 had been preserved. Some have been excavated from temples, tombs and houses and these include heads and fragments as well as reliefs, terracottas, bronze and marble models, some dating from 500 BC. Several portray the nude goddess in formalised poses, either standing or reclining, and appear to be without mythological or symbolic significance, the dove seldom being featured.

Enthroned goddess holding a dove on her lap with spread wings, from a Calabrian votive monument, c.500 BC. (by permission of the Ministero per i Bene e le Attività Culturali, Museo Nazionale di Reggio Calabria)

18

One of the most famous temples of Venus stood on the summit of Mount Eryx (Erice) in north-west Sicily. It was restored by the emperors Tiberius and Claudius as one of the great shrines of the Roman world. Among the Greeks, Sicilian doves were called "pets of Aphrodite" and it has been claimed that the Romans first learned about the domestic pigeon at Eryx. Two legendary dove journeys that took place there annually were continued by the Romans. The first, the Festival of Putting to Sea, was celebrated when the goddess with her doves was said to be visiting her temple in North Africa at Sicca Veneria, south of Carthage. This may have been one of many temple dovecotes established in the Carthaginian Empire. Nine days later the Festival of Coming to Land marked her return to Sicily

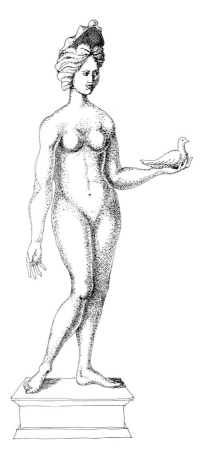

*(above left) A bronze of Aphrodite with a dove on her head.
(© copyright British Museum)*

*(above) A Greek sculpture of a nude Venus holding a dove in her hand.
(Barbara Frears, from Laurentius Beger,* Gemmarum et Numismatum Graecorum, *1696)*

*(left) The Festival of Coming to Land, celebrating the return of a dove to the temple of Venus at Eryx, from a Greek vase painting.
(from Johann Tischbein,* Collection of Engravings from ancient vases ..., *vol.3, 1791-5)*

together with her doves, the leader of which was said to be a pink bird of outstanding beauty. According to legend the return of the goddess was marked by feasts and general rejoicing among the population. A vase painting shows the dove flying towards a priestess who carries in one hand the lustral water used for purification and in the other a tray with loaves, presumably as part of a celebratory offering. Some other temples in the classical world were inhabited by so-called dove-priests and priestesses who sacrificed the birds to her and other deities as reported by the Roman poet Ovid (43 BC–AD 17): "taken from her mate the white dove is often burned on the altars of Idalious" (a Phoenician city in Cyprus). Much later, in the 15th century, such ceremonies were envisaged by a Dominican friar in a series of woodcuts illustrating an allegorical romance known as *The Dream of Poliphilus*. A scene in the temple of Venus includes the offering of a basket of doves which vividly evokes the similar tradition in the New Testament.

Ceremonies in the temple of Venus, with dove offerings, as visualised in an allegorical romance of the 15th century, The Dream of Poliphilus, *written by Fra Francesco Colonna. (Barbara Frears)*

Away from the realms of myth and legend, both Greeks and Romans seem to have been familiar with the pigeon and to have made a hobby of breeding fancy varieties as well as using them as messengers and keeping them for food. Gardens were an important feature of Roman life and recent discoveries have revealed house and garden wall-paintings belonging to villas in Pompeii and Herculaneum, which were destroyed by Vesuvius in AD 79.

20

Two wall-paintings from a garden in Pompeii, showing white pigeons, one with a dark head. (from Jashemski, Wilhelmina F., The Gardens of Pompeii, Herculaneum and Villas destroyed by Vesuvius, *1979)*

21

Doves, sometimes perched beside fountains, appear in idyllic scenes of gardens and orchards. A poem written in the 6th century illustrates the loving care that was lavished upon a tame dove belonging to the Greek poet Anacreon. The bird drank from his cup, ate from his hand, flew around the house, slept on his lyre and in the poem was flying with a message to the poet's lover. Such familiarity with the bird can be seen in a vase-painting of the same period from Apulia, while a similar domestic scene on a stone relief is now housed in the Capitoline Museum in Rome.

Wall painting from Pompeii known as 'The Boy Successus' because the words puer successus *were inscribed beside his head. He holds his pet pigeon and a domestic duck stands beside him. The pomegranate, sometimes a symbol of death, may indicate that the boy had died. (Barbara Frears, from Wilhelmina F. Jashemski,* The Gardens of Pompeii, Herculaneum and the Villas destroyed by Vesuvius, *1979)*

This innate tendency of the bird to fraternise with man was remarked upon by several writers. Philo Judaeus, in the 1st century AD, described the protection of the pigeon in the city of Ashqelon, in southern Palestine, which was a principal centre of dove-goddess worship. He wrote:

There I found an in-numerable quantity of pigeons in the streets and in every house and when I enquired the reason I was told that an ancient, religious commandment forbad man to catch pigeons or to use them for any profane purpose. Hence the bird has become so tame that it not only lives under the roof, but is also the table companion of man and is very bold and impudent.

Lucian, writing in the following century, enlarges similarly upon the subject:

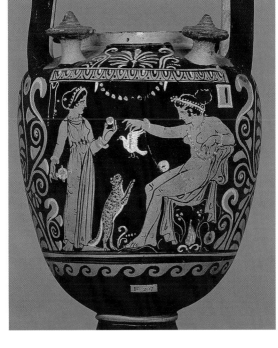

Depiction on a red-figure vase of the 6th century BC showing female figures playing with a domestic cat and a pigeon flying above. (British Museum, Department of Greek and Roman Antiquities)

> Of Birds the dove seems the most holy to them, nor do they think it right to harm these birds and if anyone has harmed them unknowingly they are unholy for that day and so when the pigeons dwell with the men they enter their rooms and commonly feed on the ground.

A bas-relief of a Roman domestic scene with two pigeons and a dog. (Barbara Frears, from Charles Daremberg & Edmond Saglio, Dictionnaire des Antiquités Grecques et Romaines, *1877-1919)*

23

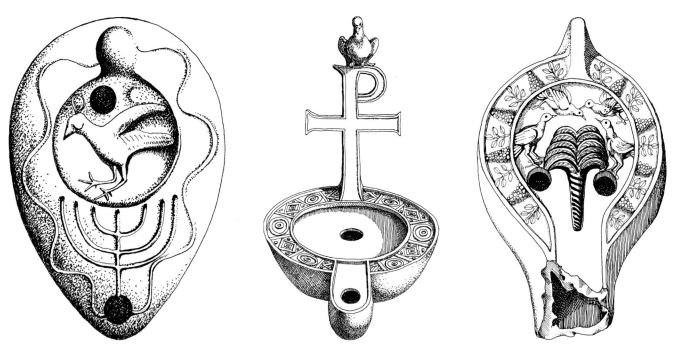

(above) Roman oil-lamps recovered from the catacombs, incorporating the dove symbol: the Jewish menorah; a Christian cross; and the Tree of Life. (Barbara Frears)
(below) Roman brooch and buckle in the form of doves.
(below right) Two Etruscan mirrors. (Barbara Frears)

This familiarity was also reflected in Roman domestic life and in several day-to-day affairs. Oil lamps were widely used, not only during life, but have been found in considerable numbers in early Jewish tombs and in the catacombs where they may have carried a symbolic meaning concerning light and life. The lamps of typical slipper-shape were made of terracotta, occasionally of bronze, the upper surface carrying inscriptions and having a central motif that was often the dove. In personal decoration the bird appeared on rings, brooches and buckles, while it was also incorporated in mythological scenes portrayed on Etruscan mirrors.

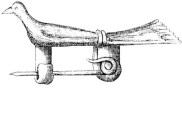

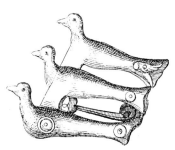

The bird appeared on sarco-phagi, steles and funerary urns, generally in the company of the deceased. In many cases the impression is one recalling the tender human bond that existed in life, but it may have been, on the contrary, that the dove represented the soul, symbolising immortality.

Coins, originating in several countries of the Near East and eastern Mediterranean, ranging in the period from 500 BC until the early centuries AD, illustrate various aspects of the dove. Greek coins, which often carry an image of a dove in flight on the obverse, show Zeus in various roles, for example Zeus being suckled by a she-goat, a dove flying overhead; Zeus at the sacred shrine of Dodona standing between oak trees on which doves perch (see page 131) and Zeus seated with his thunder-

A Greek, sculptured grave-relief showing a young girl with a pair of doves, c.455-450 BC.
(The Metropolitan Museum of Art, Fletcher Fund, 1927 (27.45), photograph © 1997 The Metropolitan Museum of Art)

bolt, a bird in flight beside him, and another pigeon on the reverse. Later Roman coins illustrate the famous Temple of Venus with two doves on the roof at Paphos in Cyprus; another shows the golden pigeon inside the temple at Hierapolis, Anatolia.

Coins depicting pigeons:
(far left, obverse and reverse) Zeus seated with a thunderbolt.
(centre) Zeus being suckled by a she-goat.
(top right) The temple of Venus at Paphos.
(bottom right) The temple at Hierapolis.
(Barbara Frears)

A Roman bronze coin depicting the dove cult at Mt. Gerizim. (Irit Ziffer)

A charm showing two doves entwined with symbols of Mars and Venus. (Barbara Frears, from Charles King, The Gnostics and their Remains, ancient and mediaeval, *1864)*

(right) Engraving from a Greek vase painting of the Heraclean Games at Thebes. The left-hand scene shows an offering of a dove being made to Aphrodite. (from Johann Tischbein, Collection of Engravings from ancient vases ..., *vol.2, 1791-5)*

An unusual, Roman, bronze coin found at Neapolis-Shekhem provides one of the very scarce clues to the Samaritan cult at the site in mid-Israel where the Samaritans worshipped the dove on Mount Gerizim. It depicts a goddess standing above the figures of Romulus and Remus with a dovecote 'hutch' on either side, from which doves emerge. Above her is the temple on the mountain top.

Many of the charms or amulets mentioned in Jewish literature have survived. They carry an intriguing mixture of motifs, ranging from the names of God, angels and patriarchs, including the dove of Noah carrying an olive branch, to images of pagan divinities, such as naked Venus with her dove and Eros; also one grotesque head that combines symbols of Mars and Venus together with two doves.

The flight of white doves liberated during the opening ceremony of the Olympic Games, the greatest of the national festivals of Greece, originally symbolised the sacred armistice that prohibited all warfare during the month of the festival. The event later became an established custom over the centuries. During the course of time, several subsidiary festivals were established in other Greek states. Thebes, for example, staged the games called Heraclean, held in honour of Heracles (Hercules). An engraving from a Greek vase-painting shows a young man crowned with a victor's olive garland offering a dove, presumably to fulfil a vow previously made to the goddess Aphrodite (Venus) in anticipation of his success. This might also have included a promise to consecrate to her service a certain number of women.

ROMAN MOSAICS

Roman mosaic work consisted of small cubes of diversely coloured stone, marble, glass and other durable substances set together in plaster or cement to produce geometrical or artistic designs. It was principally used for ornamental floors and pavements, but also for permanent decoration of walls. Remains have been found throughout the Roman Empire. Under the Byzantine Empire it became a distinctively Christian art form and was used to decorate interior walls and vaults of churches and mausoleums. Figures of the Saviour, apostles and saints, together with many creatures and plants, were worked into the decorative scheme and used to tell the Christian story. The 15th-century Florentine artist, Domenico Ghirlandaio, claimed that "mosaic is painting for eternity" and his ability as a mosaicist reflected the renewed interest in this art which was fostered by Lorenzo di Medici during the Renaissance.

The great Roman mosaic at Palestrina, dating from the 2nd century BC, was originally housed there in an ancient shrine of the goddess Isis, the great Egyptian Mother Goddess. Here, her worshippers could see on it the many sacred birds and animals dedicated to her and it can still be seen there today. It shows the Nile in flood, arising in the mountains of Ethiopia and flowing down to the city of Memphis. A vivid impression of human and animal life on and beside the river is conveyed, together with aspects of the rituals and celebrations associated with the arrival of the floods. In the lower part, a priest is seen emerging from a small shrine or temple and casting an eye on several black and white doves flying around and alighting upon an adjacent dove-house (see next page). It has been suggested that these birds might be messenger pigeons that were used to carry advance news of the flood waters.

The mosaic at Chastellux-sur-Cure, Yonne in France, was badly damaged when discovered, but details such as the dove and seashell in the centre suggest that it was dedicated to Venus. One motif of striking and unusual character, which is twice portrayed, is the dove-headed serpent, a combination of two of the traditional emblems of the ancient goddess and possibly a precursor of the scriptural tenet: "Wise as serpents and gentle as doves". Among the remarkable polychrome mosaics at the Villa Imperiale at Piazza Armerina in Sicily, built during the 2nd-4th centuries, is

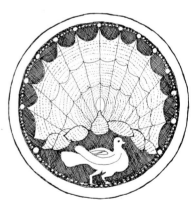

(above) Dove and sea-shell mosaic from a pavement at Chastellux-sur-Cure with motifs suggesting a dedication to Venus. (Barbara Frears)

(left) Dove-headed serpent from Chastellux. (Barbara Frears)

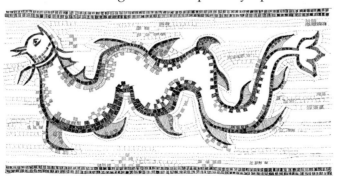

Detail from a Roman mosaic, now at Palestrina, showing a dovecote with a priest emerging from an adjacent shrine in a scene beside the Nile, c.200 BC. (Museo Archeologico Nazionale di Palestrina, photograph by Paul Hansell)

The Prize Giving to the victor of a chariot race, in a mosaic from the Small Circus at the Villa Imperiale, Piazza Armerina, Casale, Sicily. (photograph by Peter Hansell)

a scene in the Small Circus vestibule called 'The Prize Giving'. It is a parody of the spectacular mosaic in the main building, which portrays the chariot races of the Circus Maximus in Rome. The scene shows one child as the victor standing in a chariot drawn by a pair of doves and being awarded the palm branch of victory by another child.

In the early days of Christianity the Apostles were generally portrayed in human form, but they were occasionally also represented as sheep, reflecting the role played by Christ as the Good Shepherd, and more rarely as doves. The early mosaic in the 5th-century, octagonal baptistery of the cathedral at Albenga in northern Italy depicts them as doves around a circular motif containing the sacred Chi-Rho monogram made up of the first two letters of Christ's name, the Greek X (chi) and P (rho). In a later example they appear lined up on the Cross of the large

The 'Albenga Mosaic' depicting the apostles as doves from the baptistery of Albenga Cathedral, Alassio, Italy. (by permission of The British Library, from Joseph Wilpert, Die Römisch Mosaiken und Malerein, *vol.IV, 1916, LR268d2)*

29

Mosaic of the Crucifixion with doves, in the apse of the Basilica of San Clemente in Rome, c.AD 1200.

12th-century mosaic of the Crucifixion in the apse of San Clemente in Rome.

The 12th-century monumental mosaic murals in Monreale Cathedral in Sicily, built by the Norman King Roger II, used the finest Byzantine techniques, styles, compositions and iconography. They decorate the nave and crossing apses to create vast and extensive cycles of mosaics. A colossal head of Christ is enthroned in the central apse, above which is an unusual altar scene with the dove of the Holy Ghost sitting on a draped altar decorated with a cross. The later, dazzling 13th-century mosaic decoration of the Basilica of St Mark in Venice constitutes one of the greatest series of mosaics in Italy. It is based on an interpretation of fragments of the *Cotton Bible* written in the 5th century in Alexandria. In the atrium the dove appears in scenes from the Old Testament, both in the Creation of the World and in the story of Noah and the Flood.

Mosaic of Noah releasing the dove from the Ark, in the Basilica of St Mark, Venice.
(Procuratoria di San Marco, Venezia)

The discovery, in 1737, at Hadrian's Villa, Tivoli, of the famous mosaic of doves resting on the edge of a bronze basin, which was sometimes known as Pliny's Pigeons because it had been mentioned by Pliny the Elder, is now housed in the Capitoline Museum in Rome. A variation on this theme is to be found in Ravenna, where two doves are shown, but a more elaborate version from Pompeii with six birds is now in the National Archaeological Museum in Naples (see next page). Other representations of doves in this museum include one perched between two parrots on a bowl, below which a cat crouches in anticipation; also three white doves standing on and beside a cubical structure. The recovery and display of the dove mosaic at Hadrian's Villa contributed to the remarkable popularity of a new artistic genre, *mosaico minuto*, which flourished in the late 18th and early 19th centuries. Small mosaics, suitable for brooches, pendants and pins, as well as larger ones for tabletop compositions, were produced in large numbers for tourists.

Mosaic of drinking doves from Pompeii, c.AD 50.
(by permission of the Ministero per i Beni e le Attività Culturali, Museo Archeologico Nazionale, Naples)

Mosaic of the 'Capitoline drinking doves', discovered at Hadrian's Villa, Tivoli in 1737.
(Archivio Fotografico dei Musei Capitolini, Rome)

The Gilbert Collection in London contains several striking examples of drinking doves and other variations of the bird on plaques, snuff boxes and table-tops.

(top left) Brooch depicting drinking doves, in micromosaic made in Italy at the end of the 19th century. (photograph courtesy of BBC Homes & Antiques *magazine)*

(top right) Snuff-box with two doves in flight. (Trustees of the Gilbert Collection)

(centre) Bonbonnière in the form of a book, decorated with a gold-framed micromosaic of the 'Capitoline drinking doves'. (Trustees of the Gilbert Collection)

(bottom left) Table top inlaid with a micromosaic of flowers and doves. (Trustees of the Gilbert Collection)

(bottom right) Table top in malachite and marble inlaid with micromosaic, having a central decoration of the 'Capitoline drinking doves' and surrounded by monuments of Rome, c.1850. (Trustees of the Gilbert Collection)

Mosaic known as the Orpheus panel, from Horkstow, Lincolnshire, with enlarged detail below. (by permission of The British Library, from Samuel Lysons, Reliquiae Britannico-Romanae, *1813, plate 3, 743f13)*

The subject of the Orpheus mosaic was associated in Christian, as well as pre-Christian belief, with death and the life to come, which explains its appearance in many monuments of early Christian art. Examples have been discovered in widely scattered regions from Jerusalem, Algeria, Tunis, France, Switzerland, Germany and Austria, while the one discovered in Britain at Horkstow in Lincolnshire, known as the Orpheus Panel, ranks as one of the most important Roman mosaics in this country. Although damaged when discovered in 1797 it was recorded by drawings and subsequently as a set of coloured engravings by Samuel Lysons in 1799. The original is now to be seen at Hull Museum. The panel is shaped like a wheel, with Orpheus and his lyre sitting at the hub, from which radial segments join the circumference. Within each section, pairs of confronting birds, probably doves, are interspersed between an inner circle of smaller beasts and an outer procession of larger ones moving in the opposite direction. The interpretation of the theme has been taken to symbolise the sacred music of the spheres, through which Orpheus, the inspired singer, subdues the brute passions of nature.

Dove images as Christian symbols of immortality appear among the amazing 5th- and 6th-century mosaics of Ravenna, where there was great building activity after the Western Emperor moved his residence from Rome to the city in AD 403. In the mausoleum of the Empress Galla Placidia, the iconography of the 'drinking doves', sometimes called the Fountain of Life, a theme also used in Pompeii and at Hadrian's Villa, is repeated four times above the four supporting arches of the ceiling. The symbolism implied here is appropriate to the funerary message of the mausoleum, which promised life everlasting to believers. However, this symbol is adapted and derived from pagan art, the facing doves of the central feature being numbered among other facing creatures depicted similarly in Greco-Roman art and earlier. At

the Basilica of San Vitale the allegorical message of the dove is different. A pair of facing doves above a basket of fruit, together with vases holding vines, upon which three doves perch, decorate the presbytery walls. The Christian interpretation is that the doves represent not only eternal life, but also souls fed by heavenly food, while the vine symbolises The Faithful seeking refuge in Christ; "I am the True Vine" (*John* 15: 1).

Mosaics in the Basilica of San Apollinare Nuovo, built by King Theodoric the Ostrogoth in the 6th century, combine icons of his reign together with those of the Empire of Justinian. The aim of Theodoric was not to destroy, but to share the benefits of Roman civilisation; also to portray his regal, political power joined with that of Christ. The symbolism of a facing pair of doves in adoration of the Cross is a striking feature of the Basilica where they surmount an elaborate shell motif containing a suspended bejewelled crown. Twenty-eight pairs of doves also appear in the upper register of the walls of the nave above the saints and prophets.

Baptism of Christ in the Arian Baptistery, Ravenna, with enlarged detail above, showing water falling directly from the dove's beak onto the head of Christ.
(Editions Salbaroli, Ravenna)

In the Arian baptistery at Ravenna, the magnificent mosaics in the vault, which express the theology of Christian baptism, include the depiction of the dove's descent on Christ in which water falls directly from the bird's beak onto Christ's head. This contrasts with more common interpretations, in which the Holy Spirit is conjured up within rays or beams of light.

36

CHRISTIAN ICONOGRAPHY

The earliest Christians were Jews who followed the rites and teaching of Judaism and whose prophets in the Old Testament had come to expect the coming of the Messiah. The object of the first Christian apostolic missions was to persuade Jewish communities that he had arrived in the person of Jesus. These people did not portray his person, their earliest images being based on the scriptures and created out of the written letter and word signs and symbols. Since Jesus and his first followers were Jews, for whom the name of God was so sacred that it could not be pronounced, also for whom the worship of idolatrous images was forbidden, it is not surprising that there was so little truly representational Christian art in early days.

Clement of Alexandria, the Greek Christian theologian who is believed to have taken pagan images and 'purified' them, wrote in the 2nd century AD: "For we are not to delineate the faces of idols, we who are forbidden to cleave to them". But he allowed that the seal on a Christian's signet ring might depict a dove, fish, ship, anchor or lyre. The dove and fish were readily assimilated as they were already traditional symbols of the earlier goddess. The ship was recognised in several early beliefs as being the means of transporting the deceased to the afterlife. The anchor had already featured on coins of the Roman Emperors. The lyre was the instrument associated with Orpheus, the legendary Thracian poet and shepherd of classical mythology and quasi-divine musician, who charmed creatures with his playing and with whom Christ as the Good Shepherd became identified. In pre-Christian Jewish tradition, the figure of Orpheus had also been associated with David of the Old Testament. Both were poets and shepherds and both used the power of music to drive out evil spirits. The early Christians took over the image of Christ-Orpheus and substituted lambs for the original wild beasts and also enshrined the Lamb of God as the symbol of Christ in his sacrificial role. These examples illustrate how Christianity and Judaism thinly overlaid and accommodated themselves to older beliefs and customs.

The earliest truly representational Christian art is seen on the walls and tombs of the underground catacombs built about AD 200 outside the city walls of Rome, where Jews and Christians buried their dead. These comprised long corridors lined with stacked wall-tombs, which also sometimes widened into larger chambers also containing tombs. The marble slabs that sealed the tombs were inscribed with the names of the dead, together with emblems and, in Christian tombs, proclamations of faith and belief in Christ's victory over death. Early inscriptions were crudely executed, but many frescoes on walls and ceilings were elegantly framed in geometrical patterns embellished with doves and peacocks. Many of the central themes of the frescoes from the

(top) An early Christian design for a ring gemstone.
(Barbara Frears from Antonio Gori, Thesaurus Gemmarum Antiquarum Astriferarum, *1750)*
(middle) Dove and fish symbols of the goddess from the St Priscilla catacomb in Rome, c.AD 200.
(Daniel Haag-Wackernagel)
(bottom) Sailing ship and dove mono-gram from the catacombs in Rome.
(by permission of The British Library)

37

Old Testament were repeated over and over again; they include Noah and the ark, Christ-Orpheus as the good shepherd, Jonah and the whale, and the burning fiery furnace. The dove appears in several symbolic contexts on tomb slabs, wall paintings and sarcophagi. These include the motif of the facing doves either standing on each side of an urn or the Tree of Life, or carrying a swag of foliage between them. One of the most unusual depictions shows the dove holding in one claw a lighted torch with which the bird appears to be illuminating the sacred monogram. Occasionally, one dove or an affronted pair is seen pecking at a bunch of grapes; the origin of this strange and ancient alliance is both intricate and obscure. In secular art, grapes were the classical attribute of Dionysus (Bacchus), the god of wine, while Christians linked grapes with the Eucharistic wine and hence the blood of Christ; doves perching among grapes in the vine symbolised the faithful seeking refuge in Christ: "I am the true vine" (*John* 15: 1). A fine example of an outsized dove in this role is seen on a sarcophagus at Arles in southern France.

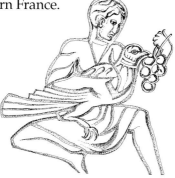

Three depictions of doves from the catacombs in Rome.
(above) The burning fiery furnace with a dove flying overhead.
(Barbara Frears from Antonio Bosio, Roma Sotteranea, *1632)*
(centre) Facing doves with a vessel between them.
(Barbara Frears from Marc' Antonio Boldetti, Osservazioni sopra i cimiteri, *1720)*
(below) Noah and a dove.
(Barbara Frears from Antonio Bosio, Roma Sotteranea, *1632)*

In the story of the Flood, the bird itself is shown with and without the olive branch in its beak, while the Ark itself is often represented on wall paintings as a simple box just big enough to hold Noah. He stands upright in it welcoming back the dove. Although the catacomb depictions generally show Noah sending or receiving back the dove into the Ark, the complete illustrated story of the bird's several journeys in the Old Testament did not appear until later. Apart from the catacombs, a more complete picture is carved on the front of a 5th-century stone sarcophagus from Trier. It depicts a crowded rectangular box, which contains standing human figures together with nine creatures, birds and quadrupeds. The dove flies overhead with the olive branch. The Flood was likened to Christian baptism by the early church fathers. It stood for the new Christian concept of the Resurrection, perhaps because converts would have already been acquainted with the early myth of the dead taking a journey by boat to the next world. Over the centuries, numerous Christian interpretations of the theme followed, including an early saying by the Venerable Bede in the 7th century: "The Ark signifies the Church, which swims through the waves of the world", while in further allegories, the Ark, sometimes replaced by a ship, symbolised man's defence against the deluge of temptation.

Noah's Ark from the 15th-century Biblia Sacra Germanica. *Note the use of a contemporary roof-top cupola or lantern. (V&A Picture Library)*

40

Noah's Ark from a 12th-century manuscript. A dove is shown being released by Noah at the top, with a raven pecking at a corpse below. Their mates are alone in their compartments in the top tier. (by courtesy of the Director and Librarian of the John Rylands Library, University of Manchester)

41

Early depictions are to be found in the medieval encyclopedia dating from 1023 which contains colourful images based on the writings of Rabano Mauro (780-850). He was the Benedictine monk and archbishop whose work contributed so much to the development of the German language and literature that he became known as the 'Teacher of Germany'. He wrote a wealth of treatises and compendia for both the clergy and the laity, as well as commentaries on all the books of the bible.

The dove not only represented Christian souls who could find no safety outside Christian belief, it also sometimes symbolised the Church itself. The Carthaginian theologian Tertullian (160-230) spoke of it as *Columbae domus*, meaning God's house. In one 12th-century manuscript it was given six wings so that it could fly rapidly through the world to propagate the gospel among all nations.

The pair of facing doves that appears on catacomb slabs, with a vessel between them and sometimes drinking from it, was interpreted by early Christians as an allegory of souls refreshing themselves with spiritual nourishment. However, earlier pre-Christian examples of facing creatures similarly portrayed confirm that this was an adaptation of a traditional image of very ancient ancestry. It was used in classical times and in Roman and Christian mosaics and in later centuries the symbol travelled far afield. In Britain, for example, a 12th-century tomb slab at the church of St John the Baptist at Lewes in Sussex and a black Tournai marble font at St Mary Bourne in Hampshire, of similar date, both carry fine representations.

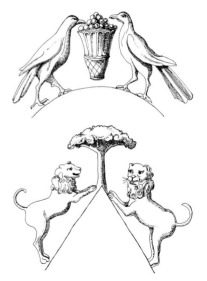

(above) Facing doves and lions. (from Raffaele Garrucci, Storia della Arte Cristiani, 1881)

(above left) Table top in pietra dura showing the 'Capitoline' doves in the centre, surrounded by shell motifs. (Trustees of the Gilbert Collection)

(far left) Tomb slab incorporating facing doves in the 12th-century church of St John the Baptist, Lewes, Sussex. (Barbara Frears)

(near left) Tournai marble font from Hampshire with pairs of facing doves on either side, dating from the 12th century, as seen in the detail below. (Barbara Frears)

(above) Part of an 11th-century tapestry of the Creation from Gerona Cathedral, showing the dove flying over the face of the waters. (Barbara Frears)

A stained-glass image of the angel Gabriel with doves, dating from 1926 and originally at Rockley Chapel, Marlborough, Wiltshire. (Stained Glass Museum, Ely Cathedral)

The use of catacomb images and motifs in early Christian art was influenced in several ways. The Constantine reconciliation between Church and State in the 4th century led to far-reaching consequences. The role of Christian art was no longer an esoteric language expressing the hopes of a persecuted minority, but had become a means of glorifying the state and church as well as being an earthly instrument of divine order. In addition, the church itself was faced with increasing pastoral duties, which made necessary some illustration of the Scriptures. As Pope Gregory the Great is quoted as saying: "That which the written word is for readers, so are pictures for the uneducated". Following earlier tradition, compositions in the Old Testament were retold as a divine story, among which were the Creation, Adam naming the animals, and Noah's Ark. The discovery in Alexandria of the charred remains of the 5th-century illuminated manuscript known as the *Cotton Bible* constituted an early example of this trend. It contains illustrations of connected cycles of Genesis, of which faithful copies survive in the 13th-century mosaic decoration in the vestibule of San Marco in Venice and also in part of an 11th-century tapestry of the Creation showing the dove flying above the waters at Gerona Cathedral in Spain. In the New Testament, by contrast, catacomb iconography was more selective in its choice of subject. Gospel illustrations first appeared in the 3rd century, in particular the Annunciation and the Baptism of Christ, in both of which the dove is a significant feature.

The words of the angel Gabriel to the Virgin Mary in the New Testament were: "Thou shalt conceive in thy womb, and bring forth a son, and shalt call his name Jesus" (*Luke* 1:31). In answer to Mary's surprise and incredulity he replied: "The Holy Ghost shall come upon thee and the power of the Highest shall overshadow thee". It is difficult to imagine a closer relationship than this between the virgin and dove as Holy Ghost which may explain why early writers, possibly also influenced by the bird's earlier role as a fertility symbol of the ancient goddess, considered it to be an erotic force as well as a heavenly messenger. The Annunciation was portrayed as early as the 3rd century in the Roman catacombs. However, it was not until after condemnation in the 5th century of the claim made by Nestorius, Patriarch of Constantinople, that Christ had been born a man and only became divine in adulthood, that she became officially recognised as the Mother of God.

The Annunciation with Saint Emidius *by Carlo Crivelli, from the 15th century, which carries both spiritual and political implications.* (© The National Gallery, London)

In art, a very rich iconography grew up around her over the centuries, possibly from the need in the Christian church for a mother figure, the object of worship that lay at the centre of many early religions. The later prevalence of the theme in Christian art reflects its doctrinal importance and explains its widespread dedication in churches, chapels and altars. The essential elements of the event are the angel, Virgin and the dove descending towards her on a ray of light that touches her head or breast. God the Father is sometimes introduced above as the source of light. Among the many depictions of the Annunciation over the centuries, the well-known Renaissance painting by Carlo Crivelli (see previous page) is of particular interest because it combines in the same work the supernatural with the natural world. It was painted for the Italian church of Ascoli Piceno in the Marches, whose patron saint was St Emidius, to celebrate the occasion on which the Pope granted rights of self-government to the citizens, which date coincided with the Feast of the Annunciation. To symbolise this coincidence, the dove of the Holy Spirit reaches Mary just as a message of the civic news is delivered by a carrier pigeon. On a bridge in the distance this is received by a citizen shown standing beside another who holds the bird. A carrying basket rests near the two men and a pigeon loft is clearly visible in the gable above them.

details from The Annunciation with Saint Emidius *by Carlo Crivelli.* (© *The National Gallery, London*)

In the 12th century, the Virgin Mary, largely espoused by St Bernard, the founder of the Cistercian Order, became an object of veneration in her own right. His famous interpretation of the Old Testament *Song of Songs* as a mystical allegory in which the bride of the poem was in reality the Virgin Mary betrothed to God, led to her being known as the Bride of Christ. Many other titles followed, including Queen of Heaven, Virgin of Wisdom, Queen of Peace, and Symbol of the Mother Church. Innumerable images showing the Mother and Child sometimes include the dove as well.

The Annunciation *by Nicolas Poussin*
(1594-1655)
(© The National Gallery, London)

(far left) Mary with a dove on her head, from an Ethiopian manuscript. (Musées Royaux d'Art et d'Histoire, Brussels)

(near left) Dove 'diving' on the head of the Blessed Virgin in an early manuscript illustration of the Annunciation. (by permission of The British Library, MS Lansdown 383, fol.159b)

47

Very little is known about Joseph, husband of the Virgin Mary, apart from what is found in the Gospels and in scenes from the life of the Virgin. According to St Jerome, when suitors of Mary brought a rod to the High Priest of the Temple, Joseph's rod blossomed. This was taken as a sign from heaven that he had been chosen. The apocryphal *Book of James* relates that a dove came forth from the rod and settled on Joseph's head and this was also illustrated in manuscripts and by artists.

On the occasion known in the Scriptures as the Presentation, when the baby Jesus was brought by Mary and Joseph to the temple in Jerusalem, "to be consecrated to the Lord", doves often featured. This continued the age-long tradition in which offerings were made in times of trouble and for propitiation and homage. In this case, however, the feeling was of gratitude and for purification and commemorated the slaying of the firstborn in Egypt, when the Jews were spared (*Exodus* 13: 11-15). This led to the Mosaic Law requiring the first-born of all living things to be sacrificed to the Lord.

The Flowering of Joseph's Rod, from an early manuscript of biblical psalms and chants.
(by permission of The British Library, Ms ADD 22279, fol.12)

Basket of doves carried at the presentation of the baby Jesus, from a 14th-century missal.
(Bodleian Library, University of Oxford, MS Douce 313, fol.260)

49

According to Luke, the Jewish rite of Purification of the mother, which required the sacrifice of "a pair of turtle doves or two young pigeons", was celebrated simultaneously with the Presentation. In scenes of the occasion, Simeon, a High Priest, to whom it had been disclosed that he would not die until he had seen the Messiah, is seen to take the child from Mary. A pair of doves, an allusion to the theme of purification, is carried either by Mary or by Joseph.

Presentation of the baby Jesus at the temple, with an offering of doves, from an early 14th-century manuscript of German origin.
(by permission of The British Library, Ms ADD 17687e)

Baptism is the right of initiation into the Christian church through immersion in water or sprinkling with it. A similar ritual was practised in the Jewish tradition, also by several early cults. Symbolically it was seen as a sacrament of cleansing and purification of the spirit. The difficulty of interpreting the Holy Spirit in tangible form must have been a problem for early artists. However, the word of the Evangelists in the Gospels to "the spirit like a dove descending" might have been a guide although there was already the ancient residual iconographic link with the early goddess and her sacred dove as symbol of wisdom. The earliest record of Christian baptism is seen in the Roman catacombs, dating from the 3rd century, in which Christ is baptised by John the Baptist using water from the River Jordan. Tertullian, writing at this time, compared Christians to little fishes swimming in the waters of baptism and many depictions include a literal interpretation of this. Early representations show the Saviour naked and either fully or partially immersed apart from the head and shoulders, but later he stands ankle-deep and water is poured over his head by the Baptist. Occasionally the dove is seen holding a vessel upside down from which the water is poured and even, as in an 11th-century miniature, the wings themselves hold it. The dove is generally depicted hovering above Christ, but as we have seen in one unusual mosaic in Ravenna water falls directly from the bird's beak onto Christ's head (see page 36). Innumerable images of the Baptism over the centuries appeared in manuscript illuminations, ivories, engravings, woodcuts, stained glass and paintings. A striking feature is the size of the dove in early works compared with many later ones. For example, the large dove carved above the 12th-century stone doorway of the Basilica of the Holy Blood in Bruges, which dwarfs Christ and the Baptist can be compared with the dove, sometimes no larger than a sparrow, which often features in the Middle Ages. Another very rare variation recorded by Adolphe Didron in 1851 unexpectedly combines spiritual and secular aspects of the bird. In this 11th-century illuminated manuscript, now housed in Lyons, but originally from the Grande Chartreuse, the dove in the baptismal scene is white with red beak and claws, but has black spots on its back and wings.

This method of baptism later led to the building of baptisteries in which early adult converts were immersed in large fonts. When infant baptism became customary, smaller fonts made of stone, granite and marble as are found in Christian churches today, became the rule. Notable examples in this country include the 12th-century stone font at St Mary Magdalene, Eardisley, Herefordshire, which was carved by local stonemasons in Romanesque style which combines Anglo-Saxon tradition with Scandinavian influence and occasional French and Italian variation (see page 54). Images on the font represent the struggle for the soul between the power of Evil and the saving grace of Christ. It is based on a vestige of the early mythology in which the

The Baptism of Christ
*by the 15th-century painter
Piero della Francesca.
(© The National Gallery,
London)*

Baptism with a dove in a
glorious aureole from a 16th-
century Book of Hours.
(by courtesy of the Trustees of
Sir John Soane's Museum,
London)

53

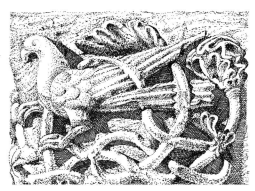

(above left) The stone font in Romanesque style by the Herefordshire School of carvers, at the church of St Mary Magdalene, Eardisley, Herefordshire. (Barbara Frears, from a photograph by courtesy of David Gorvett)

(above centre) The stone font at the church of St Michael, Castle Frome, Herefordshire, showing the Baptism of Christ and a pair of billing doves alongside. (Barbara Frears)

(above right) Dove in entwined foliage on a capital of the 12th-century Leominster Priory, believed to be the work of the Herefordshire School of carvers. (Barbara Frears)

(right) A carved wooden dove finial on the font cover at Exeter Cathedral. (photograph by Adrian Hansell)

hero descends to the lower regions to fetch back the dead, known as the Harrowing of Hell. It was a frequent subject in Byzantium as well as in the Latin west during the Middle Ages. At Eardisley, Christ with the Holy Ghost as the dove sitting on his shoulder, is shown grasping the arm of the repentant sinner, while God the Father stands by. This representation of the entire Trinity being involved in the ritual is considered unique in medieval art. A similar font at the church of St Michael, Castle Frome by the same Herefordshire carvers carries a rather different interpretation. John the Baptist, who dominates the scene, joins hands with God together with the dove's beak over the head of Christ. Two pairs of fishes with cheerful faces swim in the circular pool in which Christ stands. Alongside is a pair of billing doves, possibly symbolising the state of purity which follows baptism. Another example of the Herefordshire school is to be found on a capital of the 12th-century Leominster Priory in which a single bird stands within interlacing foliage. A later font of different style, featuring the dove, stands in Exeter Cathedral. The date of its installation is known because it was made for the christening of the youngest daughter of Charles I, born in 1644. The marble font has an elegant oak cover inlaid with figures of the Apostles and is surmounted by a dove finial. This example illustrates the problem that in the early days of Christianity, the holy water in fonts was sometimes stolen for pagan and surreptitious practices, which provoked church authorities to provide a cover that could be secured in place. A more elaborate example from 1682 by Grinling Gibbons is to be found in the church of All Hallows

by the Tower in the City of London which also has a large dove on top. An interesting modern font cover can be seen at the church of St John the Baptist, Hinton Charterhouse in Somerset. It is in the form of a church spire, elaborately gilded and having a dove with outstretched wings on the top. In English parish churches, the figure of a dove often also ornamented bench ends, as at the church of St Peter in Dyrham in Gloucestershire, and at the church of All Saints at Honington, Warwickshire.

(above) Dove carved in beech on a pew end at St Peters's church, Dyrham. (Charlotte Baden-Powell)

(above left) A carving of a dove on a roof boss of the nave at Norwich Cathedral. (Julia Hedgecoe)

Although the image of the Crucifixion was not featured in the earliest days of Christianity, the so-called monogram of Christ, which was created out of the first two letters of Christ's name, the chi-rho symbol, appeared in the catacombs. The Cross later became a central theme. At first it appeared without the figure of Christ, but this was subsequently included and innumerable other examples appeared in works of art over the centuries. Sometimes other figures were incorporated, for example, the two thieves, the sponge-bearer or the Virgin and St John. The unusual example of a Tau cross, which represents the letter T in Greek and Semitic languages, is formed as the seamless robe of Christ and depicts the crucifixion on one side with the Virgin Mary and child on the reverse. A diamond-set pendant cross hangs below in the form of a dove. Occasionally, the image of a pelican with its young, symbolising the shedding of Christ's blood to redeem mankind, surmounts the Cross, but the dove appears less often in this context.

Tau cross formed as the seamless robe of Christ in gold and enamel with a diamond-set pendant dove, possibly Spanish from the 17th century.
(English Heritage Photographic Library, The Wernher Collection)

55

In the New Testament, Christ's allegorical exhortation to his disciples, "Be ye therefore wise as serpents, and harmless as doves" (*Matthew* 10:16), had echoes of the iconography of the ancient goddess, but seems to contradict the biblical interpretation of the serpent as a symbol of evil and a synonym for Satan. However, this dual appellation was later absorbed into Christian lore. An early Roman mosaic from southern France, dedicated to Venus, includes two fine dove-headed serpents, while a later Christian capitol in Amiens cathedral consists of a pair of affronted doves drinking from a flask between them, each being endowed with a snake's tail; this has been interpreted as harmlessness at one end and wisdom at the other. Much nearer the present day, in a collection of Christian emblems, an image of the combined dove and serpent is used to represent hypocrisy. This motif might have been based on an earlier allegory called *Inside and Out*. This compares, rather tortuously, the white dove which is defined as being without bile (fault) and having an outwardly pure appearance, with the serpent representing hypocrisy and iniquity. This is likened to the human condition in which those who are endowed with true piety and simplicity must ensure that their works and deeds match accordingly.

The *Caduceus* emblem, the traditional and enduring symbol of medicine, which was based on classical and alchemical links, particularly with the god Hermes (Mercury), sometimes combined the images of dove and snake. This can be seen in a striking 16th-century representation by Hans Holbein the Younger, which is elegantly incorporated in a printer's device (see page 121). The original engraving on which this was based was entitled *Wise Innocence*. One variation of the theme arose from the ancient belief, particularly among Egyptians, that the serpent symbolised not only the underworld, but also eternity, which they sometimes represented as an encircling creature with its tail in its mouth, known as the *Uroborus*. This variation became popular from the Renaissance onwards and was sometimes combined with the dove which carried the meaning that the very end can also mean a new beginning. In religious art it was interpreted as the serpent representing eternity and the dove symbolising healing, comfort and deliverance, the latter sometimes being based on an interpretation of the dove as Paraclete or Intercessor as mentioned in the gospel of *John* (14: 26): "But the Comforter, which is the Holy Ghost". A 19th-century tomb at Lichfield Cathedral illustrates the motif, which was also used as an exterior and interior decoration at Wesley's Methodist Chapel in the City of London.

(above) The Uroborus symbolised eternity among the Egyptians and was sometimes combined with the dove.
(Barbara Frears)

Pentecost was the Jewish feast held on the 50th day after Passover as a thanksgiving for the harvest. It became one of the great Gentile Christian festivals, which marked the descent of the Holy Ghost on the Apostles and the first solemn preaching of the Christian religion. As described in the *Acts of the Apostles* (2: 1-4):

> They were all with one accord in one place. And suddenly there came a sound from heaven as of a rushing mighty wind, and it filled all the house where they were sitting. And there appeared unto them cloven tongues like as of fire, and it sat upon each of them. And they were all filled with the Holy Ghost, and began to speak with other tongues, as the Spirit gave them utterance.

The theme is uncommon in Christian art after the Middle Ages, which is surprising as it marks the birth of the church itself. Later, the festival became known as Whitsuntide and was specially dedicated to the third person of the Trinity represented by the dove. It was sometimes an occasion for performing baptism, during which the figure of a dove was customarily lowered onto the altar. A similar occasion at Orvieto in Italy, known as 'La Palombella' or the Festival of the Dove, has survived until the present day. Outside, in the cathedral square, a live, white dove on a circular frame with attached smoke flares speeds along a cable stretching from the top of the church of St Francis to a gothic structure housing

(above) A dove representing Pentecost on a roof boss in the nave of Tewkesbury Abbey, constructed in the 1340s.
(Lionel Pitt)

(left) The present-day celebration of Pentecost at Orvieto, Italy.
(Barbara Frears)

57

Depiction of Pentecost from the 11th-century encyclopedia based on the writings of Rabano Mauro. (by permission of The British Library, Miniature Sacro e Profano dell' anno 1023, *1896, KTC 38b10, tav.XIX)*

images of the Virgin Mary and the Apostles on the steps of the cathedral opposite. On the dove's arrival, numerous fireworks explode and mock flames light up the heads of the figures within. At the end of the ceremony the dove is presented to the couple who have most recently been married in the cathedral, on the understanding that they will care for the bird until the end of its life.

The doctrine of the Christian Trinity, which states that God is of one Nature, yet three persons, Father, Son and Holy Ghost, takes its authority from the gospel of *Matthew* (28: 19) and was expounded by St Augustine. From the 5th and 6th centuries, the Trinity was shown as a group in which the hand of God appeared from a cloud above the figure of Christ with a dove above him.

Depiction of the Trinity from the same 11th-century encyclopedia. (by permission of The British Library, Miniature Sacro e Profano dell' anno 1023, *1896, KTC 38b10, tav.IV)*

Sancta trinitas vnus deus miserere nobis.

The Holy Trinity beneath a baldachin or ornamental canopy, often used alone or above an altar or throne. God the Father and Christ the Son are shown holding the orb or globe, representing both as 'Salvator Mundi', with the dove flying between them. (by permission of The British Library, Ms Harley 2950 fol.242)

The Trinity woven with a circle of cloth in an allusion to the curtain of the Tabernacle from a 14th-century manuscript.
(Beinecke Rare Books and Manuscript Library, Yale University)

Variations of the theme were widely represented in early manuscripts and later works of art (see page 66). One unusual symbol described by a Rhenish mystic poet in the 14th century illustrates the concept of Trinitarian love mysticism which stressed the loving inner unity and community of the Divine Being. The surrounding cloth is an allusion to the curtain of the Tabernacle. Other examples are combined with the image of the Crucifixion as in one showing Christ on the Cross with God the Father above him holding the crosspiece in his hands, his feet resting on the terrestrial globe; the dove flies above Christ's head (see page 56).

The Eucharistic dove is the name given to one version of the metal pyx, which held the consecrated wafer of the Host. The term Eucharist means, literally, "giving thanks" and dates from the time that Jesus blessed the bread and wine which he gave to his disciples at the Last Supper. Early references describe vessels of gold, silver and copper in various forms including that of the dove. Mention is also made of keeping part of the Eucharistic bread inside the container, the Reserve, for taking to the sick and dying, particularly in the Eastern Orthodox Church. Several records and models of the Eucharistic dove have fortunately been preserved. Among examples of 13th-century Limoges enamels described in 1890, two are suspended on chains and others stand on bases. All have a hinged compartment on the back, between the wings, in which the Reserve was kept. Two unusual examples are surrounded at their base within low battlemented walls, the significance of which is unknown.

12th-century bronze, silver and gold model of a Eucharistic dove for holding the sacramental wine.
(Barbara Frears)

60

Eucharistic dove in Limoges copper and enamel, showing a hinged lid on its back.
(Rijksmuseum, Amsterdam, BK 17205)

The term Apocalypse is usually associated with the *Book of Revelation*, written by St John in AD 96 for the early Christian community of Asia Minor. This poetic work draws on the imagery of such Old Testament books as *Ezekiel* and *Daniel* and continues a certain type of Jewish and Christian literature, in the tradition of the prophets during the period from 200 BC until AD 200. Many early versions were written by Jews in reaction to oppression by foreign powers. The word Apocalypse derives from the Greek word for unveiling, which was taken to mean the hidden things known only to God. Such allegories were necessary in dangerous times when it was often safer to hide one's message than to speak plainly. The text is full of visions, images and numbers and was inspired by the twin sources of Jewish history and mystic contemplations. Much symbolism was directed towards informing and strengthening believers in the face of persecution, also to reinforcing the righteousness of God's people and the promise that Satan would be destroyed. Several themes emphasised the evils of the day and predicted a better world to come.

61

The so-called *Beatus* manuscripts were illustrated commentaries based on the Apocalypse and were originally produced by the monasteries. One of the earliest, called the *Beatus of Liebana* was made about 776 by an Asturian monk of northern Spain. This manuscript consists of passages from the *Book of Revelation*, accompanied by interpretations cast as Christian allegories. From the 10th century onwards the Apocalypse became the subject of manuscript illumination, particularly in the Catalan monasteries of northern Spain. Francis Klingender, writing in 1971, remarked upon the frequency with which birds, generally white doves, were used in these illuminations in spite of the fact that there is no specific authority in the text for their inclusion. In drawing comparison with this trend, he quotes part of the later 12th-century *Rylands Beatus*, in which the scene entitled 'Christ in Judgement with the souls of Martyrs as Birds', shows martyrs above with three rows of birds below. It is surprising to observe that the second row of birds appears to be perching above arched openings. Might these be an early indication of a dovecote, thus establishing the birds' identity?

There can be little doubt that pigeon squabs would have been a favourite item of diet among the monks and that dovecotes would have been maintained on monastery premises or farms. Another example, also from the *Rylands Beatus*, named 'The Angel's Call to the Birds', shows a highly decorative, symmetrical design, in which the angel with outstretched wings stands centrally behind the sun, surrounded by birds. These illuminations are later in date than the Catalan ones and show the undiminished vigour of design, which was followed in Apocalypses of the Romanesque period.

Among the many fantastic creatures in the Apocalypse manuscripts, those covered with eyes are exceptionally striking. In ancient times the symbolic eye was often associated with light, while in Christianity it became a symbol of the all-seeing and all-knowing God the Father. In the splendid manuscript of St Sever, written in the 11th century, there are several creatures within the 'Four Riders of the Apocalypse', which are not only 'eyed' but winged. Four angels of destruction, namely two of war and two of famine and pestilence,

The Angel's Call to the Birds from the Rylands Beatus *manuscript. (Reproduced by courtesy of the Director and Librarian of the John Rylands Library, University of Manchester)*

63

Six-winged dove covered with eyes in the 11th-century manuscript of St Sever, The Four Riders of the Apocalypse. *The dove appears to be 'shaking hands' with a haloed figure beside it.*
(cliché Bibliothèque Nationale de France, Paris)

are symbolised by four riders, the fourth being one on a pale horse whose name was Death. In this scene a white bird, whose body is covered with eyes and which has two yellow wings and two blue ones, stands centrally. This bird has traditionally been assumed to be an eagle, but it could readily be interpreted as a dove. It resembles the six-winged dove in a 12th-century manuscript, which in Christian understanding symbolised the bird flying rapidly through the world to propagate the gospel among all nations (see page 42).

Although we know that for thousands of years the dove was a symbol of the ancient goddess of fertility and that later it came to represent the Holy Ghost of Christianity, the way in which this transition and absorption took place is not entirely obvious. Over the centuries, several strands both religious and secular seem to have contributed to the story.

The discovery in ancient times of dove figures alongside or carried by images of the goddess herself has provided the chief evidence for the links between them in matters of fertility, but additional images of the bird on shrines, altars and cultic objects dedicated to her have revealed another interpretation in connection with mortality. The concept of the Great Mother as Goddess of the Dead is not out of context, because the Resurrection and future life was a dominant theme in the myth associated with her. Just as the dying year revived in springtime through her mediation so she might have been entreated on behalf of the dead for their wellbeing or return to life. This association of the dove with death on *steles* and memorials has raised the question of whether the

64

intention was to invoke the presence and protection of the deity whose symbol it was, or whether it might be meant to represent the soul of the departed. The idea of a soul-bird either accompanying the soul to heaven or returning to visit its last resting place, in the same way that a pigeon returns home, was an early belief, particularly among the Egyptians in whose art the typical soul-bird has

66

a human head. In the Near East the dove as a funerary emblem also has ancient roots and was later familiar in the classical era when Plutarch referred to it as being the bird of creation (birth) as well as of death. Greek marble *steles* from the 5th century BC, which sometimes depict doves beside effigies of the deceased, reflect this belief rather than that they were merely "pets in this life" as is sometimes claimed. The well-known Lydian

stone image of 600BC depicting the dove, the soul-bird, perched on a pomegranate, the symbol of re-birth, further supports the association. In the Roman catacombs the tradition is continued on both Jewish and Christian dedications in which the image of a dove bearing a wreath, palm branch or fillet was taken to symbolise the gift of immortality.

The sacrifice of a dove in a covenant was first mentioned in the third millennium BC on a *stele* that commemorates a treaty between two Sumerian cities in settlement of a border dispute; the pact was sealed with the sacrifice of a bull and a brace of doves. In the scriptures the most common allusion to the doves concerns its sacrifice. The bird was highly regarded by the earliest Hebrews who would neither eat nor touch it and for whom there was apparently a conflict between its holiness and its sacrifice. Sacred animals or birds, especially wild or half-domesticated kinds, such as the pigeon or dove, were surrounded by strict taboos and were looked upon as sacrosanct. In early Judaic history, particularly among the Samaritans, the dove had acquired a definite holiness and had become a symbol of the Divine Presence. Rules for raising sacrificial birds and permitted methods for killing them were included in the *Talmud*, the reference source for Jewish life, which contains civil and religious law and doctrine. The fact that the pigeon and its cousins were the only birds selected for this purpose reflects its ancient sanctity. In the Old Testament, Abraham included them in his offering when sealing his covenant with God and they also featured on lesser occasions. In the New Testament, sacrifices were made at the Circumcision of Jesus Christ and regularly at other times. It will be remembered that Christ overthrew the tables of the moneylenders and those who sold doves within the temple.

Although there are brief references to the dove in the Old Testament, very little trace of the Mother Goddess can be found, which is not surprising in the light of God's covenant banning worship of the peoples' "detestable idols". However, in spite of this, recent controversial studies have sought to show that a Hebrew goddess was recognised, particularly among mystic sects, until about 400 BC, after which time evidence of her disappears. The Hebrews called her Hokhmah, which in Greek became Sophia or Wisdom. In the Wisdom literature of the Old Testament, she was described figuratively as the "bride" of God the Father. On this basis, she is said to have resembled the ancient Mother Goddess figure of earlier cultures who, like her ancient precursors, was a powerful influence. She symbolised wisdom in its widest sense, embracing light, truth, law, insight, understanding and justice, but also more abstract qualities, such as prophesy and the interpretation of dreams. Quotations from the Wisdom literature have been adduced to betray her gender and her presence:

> Wisdom hath builded her house; she hath hewn out her seven pillars. (*Proverbs* 9: 1)
>
> Say unto Wisdom, Thou art my sister. (*Proverbs* 7: 4)

In the earliest days of Christianity, the lingering vestige of such a female divinity and her symbolic dove is vividly illustrated in the *Acts of Thomas*, which contains allusions to the "hidden mother" and "the holy dove that beareth twin young". Similarly the 1st-century Jewish theologian, Philo Judaeus of Alexandria, refers to Wisdom or Sophia as the sacred dove, which he describes as being at peace with itself.

Over the centuries, the gradual metamorphosis of the feminine dove image into the masculine Holy Ghost was partly etymological and partly doctrinal. The symbol of Wisdom (Sophia) in Greek became the neutral *Hagion Pneuma* in the abstract quality, but still personified by the dove. This in turn became the male image of the Greek word *logos*, which is the divine word that finally became the Latin *Spiritus Sanctus*. In the end, the connection between the Holy Spirit and Hokhmah and her distant origin as the Great Mother Goddess was lost except among members of the Gnostic and other heretical sects. In the writings of the Mandeans, a small, pseudo-Christian sect dating from the 2nd century AD, whose adherents still live in southern Iraq today, Eve, the mother of all mankind is known as a white ewe and also a white dove.

The popular work known as the *Legenda Aurea* or *The Golden Legend* was compiled in the 13th century by the Dominican, Jacobus de Voragine, who became Archbishop of Genoa. It relates the life of Jesus, describes the acts of the main Christian Saints and summarises, from the historical standpoint of a writer of the era, the five manifestations of the Holy Spirit. In naming the dove first, he singles out her moaning call, which he interprets as Christians wailing over their sins; "We roar all like bears, and mourn sore like doves" (*Isaiah* 59: 11). He also names the Holy Spirit as a cloud, as the breath of God and of life, as flames of fire and in the shape of a bright shining tongue, which images were often later transferred randomly to the dove itself.

A dove shown in an illuminated manuscript of a Book of Hours, the prayer book of the laity in the Middle Ages.
(by permission of The British Library, Ms ADD 17012, fol.59)

69

PATRIARCHS, PROPHETS, MARTYRS & SAINTS

The ancient, nomadic Hebrews with their herds of sheep and goats were a patriarchal people who worshipped their ancestral tribal god Yahweh. He was known as the shepherd of his people and he led them through the desert to the Promised Land of Canaan. As a warrior deity his symbol was the thunderbolt and he was believed to dwell on mountain tops and in the clouds.

Early in the second millennium BC, when Abraham and his people left Ur after the fall of the Sumero-Akkadian Empire, he took with him memories of its Sumerian culture. Much of this was passed down and enmeshed in the story and images of the Old Testament, such as the Creation and the Deluge, in both of which the dove played its part. In several early legends, life was believed to have started in the waters, which belief may have been mirrored in the line from the Creation: "And the Spirit of God moved upon the face of the waters"

(*Genesis* 1: 2), in which the dove has traditionally symbolised the Holy Spirit of God. In the story of Noah's Ark, the role of the dove is dramatic and unequivocal and has given rise to its universal symbolism of peace and goodwill. Crude catacomb inscriptions of the Ark as a simple box just big enough to hold Noah were the earliest representations of the scene, but many other variations followed over the centuries. A simple carving of Noah releasing the dove, with two of the Ark animals beside him, which is seen in the arch of the great west door of York Minster, can be compared

70

Pen and brown ink drawing on blue prepared paper by an unknown 17th-century artist of Noah and the dove.
(David Laing Bequest to the Royal Scottish Academy, RSA 278, on loan 1966 to the National Gallery of Scotland)

with more recent interpretations showing the patriarch releasing the bird without the distraction of the Ark itself and the numerous other creatures customarily aboard (*above and next page*). The figure of Noah, holding a model of the Ark, with the dove flying alongside carrying an olive branch, is another variation of the theme to be found in a stained-glass window of Jesus College Chapel, Cambridge.

71

A modern interpretation of Noah releasing the dove from the Ark, by Fred Aris. (The Portal Gallery)

The patriarchs in the Old Testament were described as the forefathers of the Israelites, including Abraham and Moses, but the list was later expanded to include King David. He was the second king of the united kingdom of the Hebrew people, ancestor of Jesus Christ and writer of numerous psalms, as quoted in the *Second Book of Samuel* (23:1): "The sweet psalmist of Israel". He was also referred to in the well-known quotation: "Oh that I had wings like a dove for then I would fly away and be at rest", which is believed to have derived from one of his psalms. He was also a great warrior and his musical ability was referred to in other books of the Old Testament. Early manuscript illuminations generally show him with his harp and a dove.

David seated on his throne, holding his harp, with the hand of God appearing from above. A dove faces him on the sceptre which he holds in his left hand.
(by permission of The British Library, Ms Cotton Tib C vi, fol.10)

*David with his harp, the dove
'diving' above his head, surrounded
by musicians and a juggler, from an
11th-century English book known
as the Tiberius Psalter, possibly
originating from Winchester.
(by permission of The British Library,
Ms Cotton Tib C vi, fol.30)*

Solomon, David's son and successor, and builder of the Temple in Jerusalem, is believed to have been the author of the Old Testament *Song of Solomon*. This brief book of eight chapters was written in the form of a lyrical love song, the main parties in which are the groom, King Solomon, and his bride, a woman referred to as the Shulamite. In its lovely garden setting and among the sexual imagery and beautiful similes of the natural world, the metaphorical dove appears:

> O my Dove that art in the clefts of the rock, in the secret places of the stairs, let me see thy countenance. (*Song of Solomon* 2: 14)

Tradition has credited Solomon with outstanding wisdom which, in the Old Testament, was portrayed as God-given. This ability is demonstrated in the story of the two harlots fighting over a child in which the King's judgement was both sensitive and astute. Occasionally, the dove, as the symbol of

Solomon, with a dove on his shoulder, in stained glass by Sir Edward Burne-Jones. (Jesus College Chapel, Cambridge)

wisdom, is shown on his shoulder, as seen in another stained-glass window at Jesus College Chapel, Cambridge.

Isaiah's prophecy that a messiah would spring from the family of Jesse, the father of David, is illustrated by the words of Isaiah in the Old Testament (*Isaiah* 11: 1,2):

> And there shall come forth a rod out of the stem of Jesse, and a Branch shall grow out of his roots. And the spirit of the Lord shall rest upon him, the spirit of wisdom and understanding, the spirit of counsel and might, the spirit of knowledge and of the fear of the Lord.

This gave rise to much iconographical interpretation in the Middle Ages. The literal image was realised in sculpture, stained glass, painting and manuscript as a genealogical tree springing from the reclining figure of Jesse. In the branches of the tree, the Kings of Judah and their descendants were represented also the prophets. At the top, most versions show Christ, who was often surrounded by seven doves symbolising the seven gifts of the Spirit. An unusual variation of the tree is a 12th-century French depiction, which illustrates the Virgin and Child with the dove above her and part of the tree below.

The eponymous *Book of Zachariah* was written in the 5th century BC by a priest and prophet born during the Babylonian captivity of the Jews. He prophesied the coming of the Messiah, and also urged his people to repent of their sins coupled with a call to finish the rebuilding of the Temple in Jerusalem. An unusual 12th-century miniature illustrates one of his visions and alludes to the seven eyes of the Lord, which are shown on a stone tablet surrounded by seven encircled doves in flight. Each eye appears to follow each dove, which seems to escape and follow a trail of fire. Inscriptions beside the birds refer to the gifts of the Holy Spirit ascribed to Isaiah, namely wisdom, understanding, counsel, strength, knowledge and fear of the Lord; pity as the seventh gift was added in the vulgate version of the Old Testament written by Jerome at the end of the 4th century.

(above) This version of the Tree of Jesse is unusual in that the main part of the tree which springs from the reclining figure of Jesse is missing and also that rather than Christ at the top, it is surmounted by the virgin and child with a dove on her head. It comes from a 12th-century illustration to St Jerome's commentary on the book of Isaiah. (Barbara Frears)

Zachariah depicted in a 12th-century miniature to show his vision of the seven eyes of the Lord fixed on seven doves in flight. (from Joseph Walter (ed.), Hortus Deliciarum, *1952)*

75

(right) Christ with the seven gifts of the Spirit as doves around his head. (by permission of The British Library, Ms Harley 2895, fol.83)

(below) Seven named gifts of the Spirit from an early manuscript. (from Louisa Twining, Symbols and Emblems of Early and Mediæval Christian Art, *1885)*

Adiuua nos quesumus domi
armis noxialibus culpis ref
tati mundane subiecti ati
tione pellamur: P.

The gifts of the Holy Spirit were often represented by doves and were frequent subjects in manuscripts and art, in which they are sometimes shown surrounding the head of Christ, or encircling the head of the Virgin and pointing towards the baby in her arms. One example appearing in stained glass at the Abbey of St Denis in Paris shows the central figure of Christ with the seven gifts as doves radiating from him with the figure of the Church on one side and the Synagogue on the other.

One of the most influential prophets in the Old Testament was Elijah, who lived during the 9th century BC and was involved in the religious struggle between the worship of Yahweh and the pagan god Baal. The prophet Elisha, who had followed Elijah and become his servant, succeeded him and inherited the spirit and authority bestowed on a prophet of God. When Elijah ascended to heaven in a chariot of fire, he fulfilled the final request of Elisha by giving him "a double portion of his spirit." This has traditionally been interpreted as a double-headed dove as can be seen in the restored 17th-century stained-glass window from Lincoln College, Oxford. A variation, in which the bird, double-beaked rather than double-headed, embraces and dominates Father and Son, can

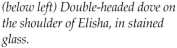

Seven gifts of the Spirit around Christ, with one sitting on his lap, from a stained-glass window in the Cathedral of St Julien, Le Mans. (Barbara Frears, from Emile Mâle, L'Art religieux du XIIIe siècle en France, 1919)

be seen in an early German biblical illustration.

(below left) Double-headed dove on the shoulder of Elisha, in stained glass. (Lincoln College Chapel, Oxford)

(below) Early German biblical illustration of a double-beaked dove, probably representing the Trinity. (Barbara Frears, from Carl Kuenstle, Ikonographie der Christlichen Kunst, 1928)

John the Baptist was the last and greatest of the prophets and the forerunner of Jesus Christ. Like Elijah, he put on a hairy cloak and retired into the desert:

[I am] the voice of one crying in the wilderness (*Matthew* 3: 3).

He made a call to moral renewal, baptism and messianic hope. The baptism was a washing away of sins, symbolising moral regeneration and repentance. At the Baptism of Christ, the Holy Ghost in the form of a dove was seen to descend from heaven. Innumerable depictions of John the Baptist and narrative cycles of his life appear in baptisteries and churches dedicated to him.

During his ministry, as recounted in the New Testament, Jesus carried out an extraordinary chronicle of healing; enabling the blind to see, the dumb to speak and the lame to walk. He also cleansed lepers, cast out demons and brought the dead back to life. An incident recorded in a 12th-century miniature shows him healing a leper in a sacrificial ritual, which involves small birds, probably pigeons. During the ritual one bird in Christ's hand is seen killed with a knife held by the leper, while its blood drips into an earthenware vessel standing beside an urn of running water. The other bird is dipped in this blood and then released, while Christ sprinkles holy water on it and the healed leper. This is a rare glimpse of the arcane, but probably commonplace ritual of ancient sacrifice, which no doubt despatched large numbers of pigeons. The Apostles also had the power to heal and baptise. Peter is recorded as having baptised the first Gentile, a Roman centurion named Cornelius (*Acts* 10: 1), while together with John the Evangelist he healed a cripple at the gate of the temple (*Acts* 31: 8).

Christ cleansing a leper who holds two birds on one arm while he sacrifices another, from a 12th-century miniature.
(from Joseph Walter (ed.),
Hortus Deliciarum, *1952)*

The early martyrs all died at the hand of the Roman Emperors so that the period before the 4th century became known as the Age of Martyrs. They were the heroes of the early Christian church, most of them dying cruelly at the stake or in the dungeon. The Greek word meaning 'witness' was given to those who submitted to death rather than abandon their faith. Their stories have been passed down in eyewitness accounts and written records through the centuries, but many embellishments have been added on the way. Stephen was the first recorded martyr who was stoned to death in the decades of the 1st century AD. Among the large number of early martyrs several remarkable virgin martyrs have been linked with the dove. The legendary Mary Magdalene who followed and ministered to Christ and was present at the Crucifixion has been considered an outstanding type of penitent and contemplative. Medieval veneration for her memory was intense and many legends became attached to her name. One manuscript illustration shows her with a white dove on her head but she is often depicted wearing the so-called Triple Crown, which was reserved for martyrs, virgins and preachers.

A dove on the head of Mary Magdalene, her hand raised in blessing on kneeling penitents including two wearing crowns. (by permission of The British Library, Ms ADD 15682, fol.144)

Although the legend of St Catherine of Alexandria is one of the most famous, there is no trace of her name in early martyr records and her story was probably composed by a Greek writer. It relates that after protesting to the Emperor Maxentius against the worship of idols and later refusing to marry him she was put into prison where she was fed by a dove; she was eventually beheaded. At the foot of Mount Sinai is the Church of St Catherine, an Orthodox monastery which contains her shrine. Legend holds that the seven lamps which burnt constantly above it were believed to contain enough oil to eat and burn and were kept alive by the miraculous visit once a year of birds, probably doves, carrying olive branches which provided the oil. A woodcut depicts the scene as imagined in the 17th century. Although Constantine had granted freedom of worship to Christians in 313, during this transitional period deities of the Roman State were still worshipped and pagan temples were still in use. For many of the populace, therefore, the dove was still sacred to the goddess Aphrodite (Venus), while for others it had already featured in the catacombs as a Christian symbol of the Holy Ghost.

(above) St Catherine in a 17th-century woodcut depicting her shrine and the seven lamps at her church on Mount Sinai. (from The Voyages & Travels of Sir John Mandevile, *1684)*

The veneration of martyrs was expanded after 313 into the much broader cult of saints, whose relics were housed in churches and whose images were represented everywhere. In the Roman courts, the definition of a saint was one who died with a reputation for sanctity, but among Christians it was more precisely defined as one who exercised the three theological virtues of faith, hope, and charity. In addition, it was expected that the cardinal virtues of prudence, justice and fortitude would be exercised in heroic degree throughout life.

The story of St Agnes, who was one of the earliest and best known of the virgin martyrs, was told in the *Golden Legend*. She was stabbed to death in Rome early in the 3rd century. Her emblem in art is the lamb, but she is also shown on a decorated, gilded glass, holding doves with rings in their beaks denoting eternity or possibly symbolising her marriage to Christ. A mural painting at the Church of St Agnes, Cawston, Norfolk, shows the seated saint receiving in her hand a ring carried by a dove.

(below) A glass engraving of St Agnes flanked by doves, each holding a ring in its beak. (Barbara Frears, from Filippo Buonarroti, Osservazioni sopra alcuni frammenti di vasi antichi, *1716)*

*St Margaret with the haloed dove in
a golden aureole above her, a fierce
dragon on the ground beside her,
depicted in a 15th-century
manuscript.
(by permission of The British Library,
Ms ADD 54782, fol.12)*

The life of the legendary St Margaret was much elaborated upon in fiction. She is believed to have lived in the 3rd century, when she underwent bizarre ordeals including being swallowed by Satan, who appeared in the form of a dragon. The story relates that the cross in her hand caused the monster to burst open so that she was delivered; this accounts for her popular role as patron saint of childbirth.

St Eulalia by John William Waterhouse, 1849-1917. The corpse is seen lying in the snow surrounded by doves. (© Tate, London, 2002)

The cult of St Eulalia, venerated in Rome at about the same time, was practised as early as the 4th century. The poet Prudentius wrote that after her death, Eulalia's spirit sprang forth from her body in the form of a dove "milk white, swift and sinless" and a fall of snow covered her dead body. Centuries later the scene was graphically painted by John William Waterhouse, but doves fly around her rather than emerging from the corpse. It is the only work in British art on this subject.

83

Legend relates that St Cecilia of Rome was condemned to death by immersion in boiling oil, which she survived, only to be killed by the stroke of a sword. She is sometimes depicted with a dove and in the Middle Ages was considered to be the patron saint of music and given the attribute of an organ, the main instrument of religious music. Later her patronage was extended to all forms of music.

Not all those who have been called martyrs died directly because of their beliefs, as for example St Scholastica, who lived at the end of the 5th century and was the sister of St Benedict and is believed to have been the first Benedictine nun. At the time of her death, St Benedict claimed to have seen his sister's spirit leave her body in the form of a dove.

A different, and more colourful example among later male martyrs, was the story of George the Martyr, which was described in Ethiopian manuscripts. The Virgin Mary, in the form of a white dove, released George from prison and then flew up in the air with him holding on to her wings.

(above) St Cecilia with a white dove and a portative organ beside her. (Rijksmuseum, Amsterdam, SK A 3306)

(right) St Scholastica wearing a nun's habit, with a book in her left hand and a dove. From an early missal. (by permission of The British Library, Ms ADD 15813, fol.225)

A collection of Ethiopian manuscripts containing
'Miracles of our Lady Mary' illustrate several
versions of one entitled 'The Virgin Mary and
George the Prisoner'. They describe the man called
George who had been "strenuously striving to
become a martyr for the sake of Christ" and who had
been imprisoned for some unknown offence.

(right) The dove is seen releasing George from
prison, with his jailer alongside.
(by permission of The British Library, 754g3, pl.LVIII)

(below) After being released from prison, George is
seen flying up into the air, holding onto the wings of
the dove.
(by permission of The British Library, Ms OR 641,
fol.111)

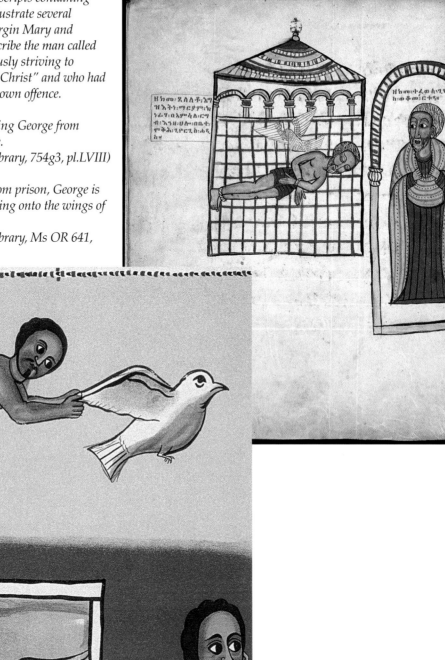

In the early days of Christianity the Four Doctors, also known as the Four Latin Fathers of the western church, were honoured as saints and theologians. They were St Jerome (c.342-420), who translated the Old and New Testaments into Latin; St Ambrose, Bishop of Milan, (339-397); St Augustine, Bishop of Hippo Regius, (354-430); and Pope Gregory the Great, (540-604). A 15th-century altar painting by Michael Pacher shows white doves as the Holy Ghost flying above, or on the shoulders of the Holy Fathers. Traditionally, however, the bird is also believed to have inspired Pope Gregory with God's words, and numerous paintings, statues, engravings and manuscript illuminations portray the scene.

(above) Pope Gregory receiving inspiration from a dove.
((by permission of The British Library, Ms Harley 3011, fol.69)

(right) Pope Gregory sitting with a white dove at his ear, in a Book of Hours. The rabbits are traditional symbols of fecundity.
(by permission of The British Library, Ms ADD 34294, fol.196)

86

Subsequently, this dove on the shoulder was imitated and transferred to numbers of other holy figures, for example St Thomas Aquinas and St David of Wales. It was even occasionally seen to inspire clerics such as St William, Archbishop of York in the 15th century. A stained-glass window in York Minster shows the facing dove, which although not actually on his shoulder, seems to be communicating directly with him.

Many early Christians became hermits and withdrew from life, often to the desert, with the aim of increasing their spiritual powers by mortifying the flesh. The foundation of monasteries was also a form of Christian spiritual expression. St Antony the Great (251-356), who was born in Upper Egypt, is claimed to have been one of the originators, based on the fact that he gathered hermits together into loosely-knit communities. Like other desert hermits, he sought God through intellectual and physical self-discipline. According to the Golden Legend, St Antony set off to find the aged hermit Paul in the desert and learnt from him that a raven had brought him half a loaf of bread daily for forty years. In 13th-century paintings the bird is sometimes represented as a dove.

The three monastic vows or counsels of perfection are poverty, obedience and chastity. They are regarded as ideals for governing the conduct of Christian monastic life. In early Christian art they were generally represented as feminine figures linked to appropriate symbols. Chastity, for example, was seen trampling on a snake or boar, which represented lust, while in secular allegory, she appears as a pair of doves denoting marital fidelity, or raising a shield to deflect Cupid's arrows. In Franciscan art the three vows were sometimes represented by the knots of the friar's girdle.

(above) St William of York who became Archbishop of York in 1140. (© Dean and Chapter of York)

(left) St David with a dove on his shoulder, portrayed in a glass engraving by John Hutton at Coventry Cathedral. (by kind permission of Marigold Hutton)

(below) St Thomas Aquinas, the great medieval doctor of the church, with a white dove on his shoulder. (Barbara Frears)

St Simeon the Elder, the first Stylite saint, was born in Syria in 388 and retired to hill-caves before taking up his position on top of a tall pillar, where he remained for 30 years. He chose this unusual way to express Christian holiness and asceticism and to dispense blessing and practical wisdom to those who visited his retreat. Two *steles* have been discovered that show the dove as Holy Ghost bestowing a nimbus on his head together with a tongue of flame. The Saint's earthly needs are seen to be provided by an attendant

on a ladder; small window-like recesses in the column exclude draughts and perhaps provide sanitation.

By contrast, the early cleric St Remigius (438-533), who was Bishop of Rheims, is chiefly remembered for having brought about the conversion to Christianity of Clovis, King of the Franks. The Saint's attribute is a dove, which appears in manuscripts, wood-cuts, prints and

later paintings, carrying in its beak a phial of oil which contains the chrism that was used when administering confirmation, customarily following the baptism of adults.

St Columba, also known as Cholm Cille, meaning Dove of the Church, was born in 521 in Donegal, Ireland, where he founded several monasteries. He is best known for the conversion to Christianity of the Picts in Scotland and the foundation of the well-known monastery on the island of Iona in south-west Scotland.

In England a medieval wall painting, dating from about 1500, of St Thomas à Becket (1118–1170), has recently been

discovered at the church of St John the Baptist in Cirencester, Gloucestershire. The saint is seen in prayer in front of the altar at Canterbury Cathedral while above him the image of God receives his soul in the form of a white dove.

In Italy, St Francis of Assisi who was born in 1182, was founder of the Friars Minor that later became the Franciscan Order. He had a great love of nature and gained the reputation of caring for birds, animals and beggars. It is recorded that he had a special affection for the lark, which was sometimes used as his symbol, but there are also tales of his love for the dove. His preaching to the birds became a favourite subject for artists as can be seen in the painting by Benozzo Gozzoli in which two white doves feature prominently. St Clare of Assisi, founder of the Poor Clares came under the influence of St Francis and is also sometimes shown with a dove flying above her.

In the 5th century, the Welsh-born St Samson became a follower of St Illtyd who founded the great Abbey of Llantwit in South Glamorgan, whose ancient dovecote still stands today. In an early account of his life there is a marvellous description of the dove that appeared during the ceremony of his ordination at Llantwit. In the words of the narrator, St Illtyd

St Francis preaching to the birds. (Barbara Frears, from a painting by Benozzo Gozzoli of 1452)

> saw a dove sent from heaven through the open window take its stand fixedly on high over St Samson, not as is the way of a bird flying or flitting about, but remaining all the time without the least fluttering of its wings while the ministers went everywhere throughout the church. And not only so, but when the bishop raised his hand over him to confirm him as deacon, that dove, sent as I have said from heaven, descended on his right shoulder and there persistently stayed all the time until the entire service was finished.

89

Innumerable other saints were canonised over the years, many being linked with the dove. St Nicholas of Tolentino (1245-1305) must be distinguished from the earlier St Nicholas who lived in the 4th century and was the patron saint of Russia and the original Santa Claus. Numerous miracles were attributed to the former saint, one of which tells the tale of the resurrection of roast pigeons that took to flight during a meal. He also founded a charity known as 'St Nicholas Bread', which was given to the poor and women in labour.

St Peter of Alcantara (1499-1562) was born in Spain and became a Franciscan friar and the outstanding mystic of his age. He established a reformed Franciscan Order and preached poverty, austerity, solitude and contemplation. An engraving shows him looking up towards the white dove above his head.

St Theresa of Avila (1515-1582) was a Spanish mystic who was much influenced by St Peter. In her middle age, as Mother Theresa, she founded Carmelite convents which later spread to many parts of Spain. In them she restored the strict discipline of the original order with daily mental prayer as part of its rule. She had an attractive personality which combined practical common sense with a markedly mystical imagination. The 17th-century writer Richard Crashaw's reference to the "eagle and the dove" in her character has become proverbial. Like other saints who have left important written works, she is often seen to have been inspired by the Holy Ghost in the form of a dove, as can clearly be seen in the painting by the Flemish painter Peter Paul Rubens.

(above) St Nicholas of Tolentino and the miracle of the resurrection of the pigeons in Constantinople in 1748. *(Barbara Frears)*

(right) Teresa of Avila's Vision of a Dove, *by Rubens.* *(Fitzwilliam Museum, Cambridge)*

BESTIARY & FABLE

A lengthy allegorical work known as the *Physiologus*, designed to teach Christian doctrine by way of animal legends, originated in Alexandria in the 2nd century. It was not translated into Latin until later and did not reach Europe until the 12th century when it became one of the leading picture books of the era. The influence of Greco-Roman culture upon it, including the works of Pliny and Aristotle together with oriental ideas and the fauna of North Africa, combined to produce a remarkable amalgam, which later gave rise to the *Bestiarium* or bestiary. With the exception of the Bible, no other early Christian work has been so popular or been translated into so many languages.

In addition to descriptions of animals, birds and fish, both real and mythical, such as dog and dragon; pelican and phoenix; owl and basilisk, the *Physiologus* also includes mention of stars, planets and stones. The accompanying text is devoted to theological allegories, many of which now seem far-fetched and tortuous. The pattern for each section generally follows three main headings, a quotation from the scriptures, facts of animal history and a moral to be drawn for human life. However, progressive changes led to a reduction of the scriptural content and increasing emphasis on nature, although attention to moral instruction was retained. It has been suggested that such later versions might have been intended for the monastic lay brethren.

One of the special versions of the bestiary, devoted to birds and entitled the *Aviarium*, is attributed to the French prior Hugh of Folieto and dates from the 13th century. The dove is given pride of place in it, occupying far more space than that given to any other bird. This text is often referred to as the 'silvered dove', because it elaborates upon the biblical quotation:

> Though ye have lien among the pots, yet shall ye be as the wings of a dove covered with silver, and her feathers with yellow gold. (*Psalms* 68: 13).

The dove is said to stand for the church, the faithful, the prelacy and the preachers. In a later interpretation the bird's silver wings are said to symbolise eloquence, while the golden feathers are likened to the brightness of love and charity.

The final chapter of the *Aviarium* enumerates ten of the dove's characteristics, all of which were based on close and accurate observations of the bird, akin to those described by Aristotle. Its song is a mournful plaint; it lacks gall; it continually kisses; it flies in flocks; it does not live from plunder; it collects the better seeds; it does not feed on corpses; it nests in the holes of rocks; it sits on streams in order to see the shadow of the hawk, which it can then quickly avoid; and it has twin young. Among the allegorical Christian lessons drawn are the twin young, signifying love of God and neighbours; the dove resting beside

91

The habits of doves as illustrated in the 13th-century Alnwick Bestiary. Here one can see the osculo amore – "they kiss and bill together before their treading". (by permission of The British Library, Ms Royal 12 C XIX)

streams symbolising the man who reads the scriptures in order to avoid the wiles of the devil; the bird building in holes of rock representing the one who places his hope on the wounds of Christ's Passion; and in collecting the best grain and seeds, the doves are likened to preachers who select the best sentences from the scriptures.

A geometrical *schema* incorporating a central dove motif appears in several *Aviarium* manuscripts. This singular type of diagram has been traced back to antiquity and was designed as a means of demonstrating relationships between the physical properties of things in the material and natural worlds as well as between abstract ideas. Sometimes named 'The Moral Exposition of the Dove' this example incorporates several homilies including the silver dove quotation together with other Biblical references.

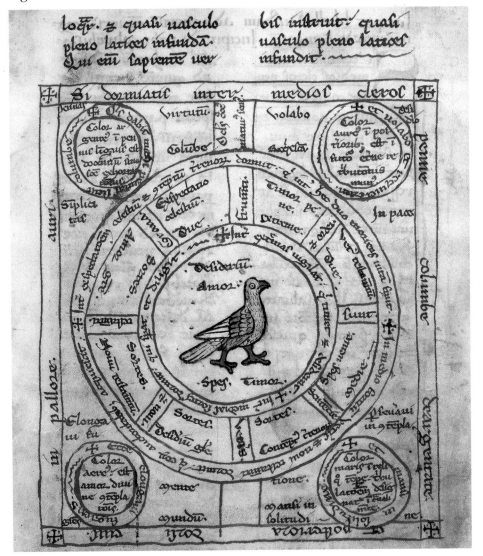

Doves from a 13th-century manuscript of the Aviarum.
(left) A central dove is seen in a moral schema with allegorical interpretations and attributes of the dove from the scriptures.
(above and below) Doves decorate other parts of the manuscript.
(all images © The J. Paul Getty Museum, Los Angeles)

93

The Perindens tree.
Doves are seen perching
on the branches and on
the dragon' tails.
(Queen Mother Library,
University of Aberdeen,
Ms 24, fol.65)

ne poſtquam accepıs ſp̄m ſc̄m voc eſt ſpūalem columbam
ıntelligıbılem de celo deſcendentem er manentem ſupте foпs
fıaf ab ет̄nıtate. aıenuſ a pтe̅ er filıo er ſpū ſc̄o. er dтaco тeın
теrımat .ı. dıaboluſ. Нam ſi тu habeaſ ſp̄m ſc̄m non poteſt т̄

94

Several bestiaries refer to a tree called *Peridexion* or *Perindens*, which was believed to grow in India and to produce sweet fruits on which doves fed. In some manuscript illustrations the birds are certainly pigeon-like and in the original account they may have been a variety of fruit-pigeon rather than the rock pigeon, which does not feed on fruit. In one English version, the tree is recognisable as an oak complete with acorns. Legend held that the doves were protected from their enemy, the dragon which lurked on the ground below, as long as they stayed in the tree or within its shade. Christians interpreted the tree as either the Church or God the Father; the doves eating the fruit as the Holy Spirit acquiring heavenly wisdom; and the dragon as the devil. The intended message was that those who remain in the Catholic Church and possess the wisdom of the Holy Spirit would be safe from the wiles of Satan.

From the 12th century onwards, bestiaries were increasingly interpreted in a secular sense, although they were still a source of moral edification. In England, Alexander Neckam wrote a manual, *De Naturis Rerum*, in which he projected human qualities onto creatures of the living world, as in the fable tradition. For him, nature became a mirror of human life from which moral lessons could be learned. The work of Bartholomew the Englishman, a 13th-century Franciscan friar, writing *On The Properties of Things*, also demonstrates the trend away from a theological interpretation. Like Neckam, he describes birds, beasts and fishes under their appropriate elements of air, earth and water and uses observations about them to point out moral messages. He wrote on a grander scale than Neckam and described his own 19 books as elementary texts "for young scholars and the general reader", but they became standard references at universities both in Britain and throughout Europe. Writing of the pigeon, Bartholomew says:

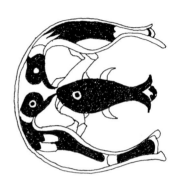

> The culver is the messenger of peace, the example of simpleness, clean of kind, plenteous of children, the follower of meekness, the friend of company and the forgetter of wrongs.

Established western monasteries maintained contact with the older ascetic communities of Syria, Palestine and Egypt from the time of Charlemagne. Imports from such sources of Coptic and Asiatic designs, particularly fabric, were influential because Hellenistic forms and motifs had already been translated into half-barbarised idiom. Such influence is reflected in the fantastic bird and fish initials which are found as embellishments of Merovingian manuscripts.

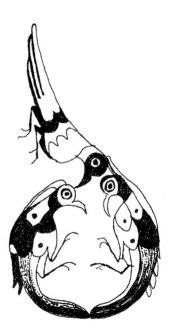

Illuminated capitals from an early Merovingian manuscript. Merovingians were a Frankish dynasty of the 5th-6th centuries AD. (Barbara Frears from Paul Lacroix, The Arts in the Middle Ages and at the Period of the Renaissance, *1870)*

The fable was closely allied to allegory and the bestiaries. The beast fable originated in lands in which ancient animal worship once prevailed, such as Egypt, India and Africa. An example from ancient Egypt in a satirical papyrus shows a lion and a unicorn playing chess. The earliest Greek fables were attributed to Aesop in the 6th century BC, the tradition being preserved later by word of mouth. A freedman named Phaedrus in the reign of Augustus, translated the fables into Latin verse interspersing them with anecdotes of his own; a prose version written in about the 10th century served as a model for medieval fabulists. Their earliest purpose was to teach rhetoric and ethics and later to instil simple lessons of prudence. By contrast with the *Physiologus* and bestiary allegories, they generally lack Christian overlay, but the essence of the fable in showing that animals often behave like humans, with all their wisdom and folly, approaches the morality of the bestiary. Several early collections allude occasionally both to the classical deities, such as Zeus and Hermes, as well as to the god of Christianity. The earliest pictorial English version of Aesop's fables was embroidered on the top and bottom margins of the Bayeux tapestry in which

Details from the Bayeux tapestry, showing facing doves in the borders. (from Eric Maclagan, The Bayeux Tapestry, *1943)*

various Anglo-Saxon artists recorded their own country's conquest by the Normans. Several fables, such as those of the Crow and the Fox, and the Wolf, the Goat and the Lion, have been identified, but others, such as that of a juggler wrestling with a bear, are less easily recognised. The pairs of facing and opposing birds which appear above and below the pictures of King Edward and King Harold are also unaccounted for, but they may follow the long tradition of the facing bird motif (see page 43) and are probably pigeons.

Fable of the Dove and the Serpent, illustrated by Heidi Holder. (from Heidi Holder, Aesop's Fables, *1981)*

The fable follows a characteristic form in which the lesson of morality or prudence is either implicit in the story itself or is made as a separate statement. The tale of the dove which rescues a drowning ant and is later repaid when the ant stings a fowler intent on killing the bird, draws the moral: "One good turn deserves another." The fable of the dove and snake as two main characters recalls a very ancient association, but teaches the new lesson that good can come out of evil. The story tells of a snake, which inadvertently warns a dove that is being pursued by a hunter, hence: "Even our worst enemies may help us without meaning to."

Domesticated pigeons are the subject of several fables in which the instinct of hawks and falcons to prey upon doves and pigeons is epitomised. In the fable of the Kite, Hawk and Pigeons, the dovecote birds having sought protection from their persecutor, the kite, by installing the hawk, merely exchanged one hazard for another. Under the title of the Vulture and the Pigeons, a fable told by La Fontaine with illustrations by Gustave Doré, the pigeons intervene to bring peace to warring vultures who then ungratefully turn upon them and kill them. It is conjectured that the dove as the symbol of political peace in the contemporary adage 'Hawks and Doves' has its roots in such fables.

The fable of the Daw and the Pigeons tells the tale of the jackdaw, which painted itself dove-coloured and joined the dovecote birds to share their food and comfort, but was discovered and chased away when he cried "caw", the Victorian moral drawn being: "He that trims betwixt Two Interests, loses himself with Both when he comes to be detected for being True to neither."

Fable of the Jackdaw and the Pigeons,
in a drawing by Randolph Caldecott,
1880.
(V&A Picture Library)

Lastly, there is the story included in the Indian fables of Pilpay, as well as in versions of La Fontaine and in one Russian collection, of the white dove Heeresk in which a moral is drawn, contrasting domesticity and wanderlust. The bird flies away from the nest and in its journeys encounters many dangers and disasters, but eventually returns chastened to enjoy the comforts of home.

Although many fables were familiar in Italy and elsewhere from the 11th century, it was not until the

13th century in England that Odo of Cheriton wrote his collection of fables and beast stories, many of which were derived from earlier sources. In addressing wider social issues he was unsparing in his criticisms of the

many injustices and vices of his time. He elaborated upon this in the fable called 'Of the Sparrowhawk, the Dove and the Duke', *duc* being the French name for various species of owl. It relates how the doves appealed repeatedly to the duke for help in stopping the predations of their enemy, the sparrowhawk, but his only answer was "Clok", so they labelled him a fool and a deceiver.

(above) Wanderlust versus domesticity, the tale of a roaming pigeon in a version engraved by Auguste Delierre.
(Barbara Frears from The Fables of La Fontaine, *1884)*

(above left) An illustration by William Dickes for a Russian version of the wanderlust fable, published in 1870.
(from The Pigeons, *SPCK, 1870)*

(left) The allegory of the owl in the fable of The Sparrowhawk, the Dove and the Duke. The owl is seen being mobbed by the other birds.
(by permission of The British Library, Harley 4751, fol.47)

99

An owl being mobbed by birds in a woodcut by Albrecht Dürer. (from Willi Kurth (ed.), The Complete Woodcuts of Albrecht Dürer, *1927)*

This is likened to poor men claiming justice from kings and great lords for their injuries, but who also only answer "Clok". An additional allegory claims that the duke's behaviour explains why other birds mob him, so that the owl never dares to fly out except by night. The pastime of 'owling', which enjoyed a brief vogue in the 18th century, exploited the tendency of birds such as pigeons to mob owls in daylight. In practice, a trained owl on a string was made to perch on top of a pole; limed crossbars lower down entangled the mobbing birds so that they were easily caught. A similar custom was prevalent in the Himalayan region until recently and is painfully reminiscent of the current Mediterranean practice of netting or shooting migratory birds, which have been cruelly trapped on limed branches.

The sport of owling in England in the 18th century. (Author's collection)

A century or so ago, Eugène Goblet, Count d'Alviella, claimed that many of the familiar symbols of antiquity had arisen in India, but there are few references in that nation's diverse and complicated mythology to the dove being used in this way. However, occasional references come to light suggesting that over the centuries the bird has featured both symbolically and artistically. In traditional Islamic belief the throne of God has four pillars, each supported by an angel. An early depiction shows the angels supporting a canopy with rows of doves.

Doves depicted in a canopy
supported by angels,
from an Indian manuscript.
(Bodleian Library, University of
Oxford, Ms Pers. d. 29, fol.66r)

101

This gives a glimpse of their ethereal role, while an 18th-century miniature painting from Rajasthan entitled 'Lady watching Pigeons mating' illustrates

Watching domestic pigeons for pleasure in India. Note the dovecote at ground level and the mating pigeons, enlarged above. (Bodleian Library, University of Oxford, Ms Douce or. d. 3, fol.10r)

their domestic appeal. One of the most interesting early accounts of doves comes from the Indian text *Ain-i-Akbari*, written by Abu Fazl, which chronicles the administration of the great 16th-century Mughal emperor Akbar, a keen pigeon fancier. His pigeons, to which he was devoted, accompanied him on his travels, transported in small cotes as seen in several 17th-century Mughal miniature paintings, some of which also beautifully illustrate varieties such as Lahores, Fantails and Nuns.

The fables of Pilpay, who is described as an ancient Indian philosopher, were written in Sanskrit during the 3rd century and translated into Arabic

(below left) Watching domestic pigeons from a contemporary Indian miniature.

(below right) Several varieties of Indian pigeons, including Lahores and Fantails, with a portable dovecote, from a Mughal miniature dated c.1670.
(© Copyright British Museum)

103

(left) Varieties of Indian pigeons on a hillside, with a portable dovecote. (Fitzwilliam Museum, Cambridge)

(right) A pair of pigeons, possibly Lahores, beside a portable cote. (by permission of The British Library, Ms ADD OR 3129, fol.31)

for the emperor Akbar in the 16th century and finally into English in the 18th century. They were once extant in 20 languages and became as popular as those of Aesop. Pigeons feature in several of his stories, including one entitled 'The Raven, the Rat and the Pigeons' or 'The Advantage of the United Action of Friends'. In this early allusion to team spirit, several pigeons trapped by the fowler's net are exhorted by their leader, a wise old pigeon sometimes called 'The Prudent', to work together to loosen the net so that they can all fly away although still entangled in it. Having landed out of harm's way, the leader asks a rat to help him to "free my companions before me". Admiring his selflessness the rat nibbles a hole in the net and frees them all. As a sub-plot, the cunning raven plays the role of a hidden observer who, wishing to discover the secret of the rat's co-operation, but being unaware of the latter's respect for the pigeon, fails to gain a similar confidence.

Pilpay's Fable of The Raven, the Rat and the Pigeons:

(above left) The pigeons are entangled in a net in the sky, watched by the fowler.
(by permission of The British Library, Johnson 54, No.19)

(above right) The pigeons are being freed by the friendly rat.
(by permission of The British Library, Johnson 54, No.20)

(left) The rat is seen nibbling at the net to free the pigeons, watched by the Raven.
(Bodleian Library, University of Oxford, Ms Pococke 400, fol.82v)

Another early trace of the dove is found in a Buddhist relief from the 3rd century, which depicts an Indian legend concerning the great and virtuous King Usinara who sacrificed a limb for a pigeon. In this story, the bird sought his protection from a hawk, which in its turn argued his own case for preying on it as being part of his diet and of his nature. The king, finding himself in a dilemma, offered to cut off a piece of his leg equivalent to the weight of the intended victim. The moral of the tale is drawn at the beginning by two gods who were sent as two birds in disguise to test the king's virtue and wisdom. This fable of mercy concludes on a happy note; the birds revert to their true form and all praise the king. Today, a mural depicts the scene at the Jain Bird Hospital in India, which is located opposite the Red Fort in Delhi. The Jains, the practical side of whose philosophy is non-violence towards all living things, founded this bird sanctuary in 1929. In 1999 they treated 29,899 individual birds, most of which were pigeons.

A modern depiction of a Buddhist relief from the 3rd century depicting the legend of King Usinara who sacrificed his limbs for a hungry hawk. The severed limbs are seen in the balance, while the hawk looks on below. Note the reference to the Jain Bird Hospital at the bottom right. (photograph by Amar Grover)

SYMBOLS & ALLEGORY

A symbol need not arise from any one source, but can adapt or respond to different ages, religions, cult or civilisations. It may have meaning, may reveal, or may conceal.

In Greek philosophy, Pythagoras voiced the concept of virtue and vice as opposing forces in the 5th century BC. This idea was adopted by the early Church which, together with several early sects such as the Gnostics and Cathars, shared the belief that evil must exist as a counterpart to good. This concept was illustrated in the *Psychomachia* by the 4th-century AD Spanish poet Prudentius, an allegorical work also called the *War of the Soul* or the *Battle of the Vices and Virtues*. It recalls the well-known tradition in classical antiquity of depicting the human figure, generally female, as an abstract idea such as Peace, Fortune, Fame and Winged Victory, the latter thought to have been based on a statue of Venus. The *Psychomachia* depicts combats between armed female figures in the widest sense with examples such as the battle between concord and discord; charity and avarice; faith and idolatry; humility and pride; and chastity and lust. Sometimes, Prudentius personified opposing forces of the soul as a female figure called Sophia, also known as Sapientia Dei, or Holy Wisdom who stemmed from the ancient Mother Goddess with whom she shared the dove symbol. She was also known as Hokhmah in the Gnostic tradition and as the Shekhinah in Jewish belief. In the early days of Christianity, Sophia occasionally became identified with the Virgin Mary who is shown in a 12th-century manuscript on the Lion Throne with the Divine Child, holding a staff surmounted by a lily

A Greek manuscript showing Sophia, also known as Holy Wisdom, and Prophetia on either side of King David. Prophetia, who represents another aspect of the early Goddess in her ability to prophecy, points to the book which David holds. (cliché Bibliothèque Nationale de France, Paris)

107

and a dove. Even more unusual is an illustration of Christ called Sancta Sophia in a manuscript of the same period.

The Jewish philosopher Philo of Alexandria, writing in the 1st century AD, exemplified the Hellenistic tendency to identify animals and birds with the virtues and vices as in the fable tradition. In his allegorical interpretation of the story of Noah, he likened the waters of the Deluge to streams of passions and desires which seduced the Raven, but were rejected by the virtuous Dove that returned to the Ark. It was a short step from these views to ascribing figurative meanings to the birds, the raven representing vice and the dove embodying virtue. He also described the dove as being a tame and sociable bird that "frequented the cities of men and was pleased to dwell with mortals". This has a familiar ring nearly two millennia later and echoes the problems of today's feral pigeons.

The Renaissance in 14th-century Italy was characterised by a growing interest in the classical past, both its literature and its ancient remains and this formed the basis of the humanist movement. That is not to say that antiquity had been a closed book in preceding centuries, but it had been seen chiefly through the eyes of Christian belief and was discouraged by the Church Fathers who urged the populace to turn to the gospels rather than classical myth. During that time the tendency had been to treat the ever-popular pagan myths as allegories with moral and spiritual meanings below the surface. However, as early as the 6th century, Fulgentius, Bishop of Ruspa in modern Tunisia, produced his series of *Mythologiae*, a work which made pagan lore and literature palatable to Christian views. In it he described the deities of classical antiquity and emphasised not only their traditional attributes, but also the hidden meanings of the myths. For example, in telling of the goddess Venus as being a symbol of the life of pleasure, he explained that doves are placed under her patronage "for the reason that birds of this species are fiercely lecherous in their love-making." Among other examples, the god Mercury had the title of protector of businessmen "for the reason that he has feathered heels, because the feet of businessmen are everywhere in a rush as if winged".

The writings of Fulgentius later influenced Giovanni Boccaccio, the 14th-century Italian poet whose *Genealogy of the Gods* also elaborated upon the pagan divinities. In one edition of the work he refers to Venus as "Venus in bono et in malo" and this concept of embodying universal love and harmony as opposed to profane or erotic passion became popular in renaissance Italy. In Christianity it was interpreted as divine love or charity (*caritas*) as contrasted with earthly love (*cupiditas*). In another edition a woodcut shows Venus holding

(above) Venus and her doves from an early manuscript entitled The Failure of Love.
(Barbara Frears from Guy de Tervarent, Attributs et symboles dans l'art profane, 1450-1600, *1958)*

(left) Venus, Cupid with his bow and arrows, the three Graces, and a pair of doves perched on a slate.
(from Giovanni Boccaccio, Genealogia, *1531)*

a slate, above which two of her doves are flying; also included are the Three Graces, attendants of Venus who, with her, personified grace and beauty, together with blind-folded, winged Cupid with his bow and arrows. In Greek mythology he was thought of as the son of Venus and personified love. He is often shown with a blind-fold, not only because love is often blind, but also in Christian allusion to the darkness that was believed to be associated with sin. The curious inclusion of a slate was apparently due to an etymological confusion in an early translation of the original manuscript in which *concam marinam*, meaning seashell or scallop shell linked with Venus, was mistranslated as slate.

In the Renaissance, one of the chief leaders of the humanist and antiquarian movement was Francesco Petrarca (1304-74), who held the fervent conviction that classical antiquity was a light that had been extinguished by scholastic teaching in the Middle Ages. His allegorical poems called the *Trionfi* were

Venus in a chariot drawn by doves. (Barbara Frears from Guy de Tervarent, Attributs et symboles dans l'art profane, 1450-1600, *1958)*

based on Roman victory celebrations and processions, often featuring the pagan gods, but sometimes also carrying religious allegorical interpretations. One of the most popular subjects was the Triumph of Love in which Cupid (Eros) rode in a chariot drawn either by white horses or goats, while Venus was pulled by doves or sometimes accompanied by them in flight. The theme occurs in 15th- and 16th-century Italian painting at a period when civic processions often celebrated the triumph of pagan divinities. Sometimes images of the victors were interpreted in astrological cycles, each month being represented by its reigning planetary deity; Venus was the name given by the Greeks to the second planet from the sun, the morning or evening star.

The story of the love affair between Mars and Venus was familiar in Greek mythology and was often represented symbolically by the dove and helmet emblem. In the Renaissance their mythical relationship was made into an allegory of strife overcome by love, in which Mars was shown to be a lover as well as a warrior. One version of the myth describes the union giving rise to an offspring named Harmony or Concord. The idea that opposing forces of Love and Strife, when united, might give rise to the birth of such a child was familiar to classical writers and was sometimes symbolised by facing doves. Furthermore, a pair of facing or billing doves had represented fertility and fecundity as attributes of the early goddess and this came to mean love and constancy in later times.

Framed billing doves in the centre of a drawer, detail from an 18th-century Japanese lacquered table. (reproduced by permission of the Trustees of the Wallace Collection, London)

On ne doit priser vint fardon
moy ne mon art ne mon brandon

Comment fix ieunes colomba
en vnt char qi fut riche et beaux
maimenent venus en lost damo?
pour lui faire hastif secours

L orefit la mestme appella
son char comanda astella

*Venus and Mars. The goddess is
seen in a chariot drawn by doves
with helmeted soldiers in the
foreground, representing Mars.
(by permission of The British Library,
Ms Harley 4425, fol.138)*

111

A subsequent interpretation by the Italian painter, Giovanni Battista Tiepolo, once called the last painter of the Renaissance, is his *Allegory of Venus with Time* (1754). It was painted for insertion into the plaster ceiling of the Contarini Palace in Venice. The scene shows Venus having descended from her chariot in the clouds with the Three Graces beside her, a pair of billing doves above her and winged Cupid with his quiver of arrows below her. She is handing a newly-born child into the arms of winged Chronos, or winged Time who, having put down his scythe, represents time rather than mortality. The significance of the scythe arose from an early Greek confusion between Chronos, meaning time, with Cronus, their old god of agriculture whose symbol was the scythe. It has been suggested that this work, with its erotic symbolism of Venus and Cupid might have been intended for a bridal ceiling in joyful anticipation of a hoped-for child. Another possibility is that the myth of Aeneas, the child of Venus and legendary founder of Rome, formed the basis of a claim that he was an ancestor of the Contarini family.

Oil painting by Jan van Bijlert, Dutch, c.1630-40, showing Venus chastising amoretti (a diminutive of amor or love, representing Cupid), with a pair of white doves alongside. (Chrysler Museum of Art, Norfolk, Virginia, Museum Purchase, 2002.1)

Tiepolo's Allegory of Venus with Time. *Venus, with a pair of billing doves above her, hands the child to winged Chronos or Time. Detail of the doves below. (© The National Gallery, London)*

Venus and Cupid with a pair of doves *by Annibale Carracci, 1592. (Galleria Estense, Modena, photograph by Pincelli Foto)*

Early in the 15th century Marsilio Ficino, the scholar, philosopher, priest and humanist, who was tutor to Cosimo di Medici, in attempting to reconcile the principles of Christianity with classical myth, proposed that Amor or Love should be regarded as a philosophical principle on the basis that it was the oldest of the gods and had existed even before the world began when all was chaos. He also extolled Venus as being the goddess who personified humanity and embraced a multitude of virtues while epitomising beauty both in herself and in nature. This opened a whole new genre of so-

called treatises on love, in many of which Venus and her doves played a central role often in the company of Cupid. In early classical times Eros, once known as Son of Chaos, was subordinate to Venus, but his importance gradually waned until he finally played the part of a wayward and mischievous winged youth who shot arrows of infatuation and desire at random into his victims. He is widely represented in Renaissance and later painting and sculpture, generally symbolising erotic love, but often merely serving as an emblematic reminder of the theme.

Portrait of Nell Gwynne, mistress of Charles II, as Venus, with her son Charles Beauclerk as Cupid, and a pair of billing doves, by a follower of Peter Lely, 17th century. (Army and Navy Club, London, UK/ Bridgeman Art Library)

The principal theological virtues outlined by St Paul (*Corinthians* 13: 13) were Faith, Hope and Charity, while the four cardinal virtues – Justice, Prudence, Fortitude and Temperance – were formulated by Plato as qualities required by citizens of the ideal city state (*Republic* 4: 427). In the Middle Ages the Church Fathers combined these as a cycle of seven virtues, sometimes paired with appropriate vices, which together were widely represented in medieval manuscripts, sculpture and frescoes. A 12th-century illuminated manuscript, believed to have been made for a Dominican friar, illustrates one version of this type of moralising. It depicts a Christian knight in the role of Christ, armed with seven virtues symbolised by his horse and saddlecloth together with his sword, shield and helm. Above him is an angel bearing banners representing the virtues of Poverty, Gentleness, Struggle with Sin, Desire for Justice, Mercy, Pureness of Heart and Peace. These are interposed behind seven images of the white dove in a line facing and combating the seven vices opposite.

The tendency to increase the original seven virtues was occasionally combined with the addition of some of the seven gifts of the Holy Spirit, even expanding the number to twelve to correspond with the number of apostles. The relation of symbolism to medieval church architecture whether in early mural painting and later in sculpture painting or stained glass had been customary since the mid-12th century. Its purpose was to embellish some features of the church building which was itself felt to be a visual embodiment of the spiritual church. In the 13th century an architectural exposition of the virtues and vices decorated the central porch of the cathedral of Notre Dame, Paris, where the twelve virtues as female figures sit below the apostles. They demonstrate a convention of the time, in which each figure holds a circular disc bearing a symbolic device that enables identification to be made; they are otherwise practically indistinguishable. Thus, Humility bears a dove and Prudence is represented by a snake. In Chartres cathedral a variation of the theme is found in effigies based on St Anselm's 11th-century interpretation of the Beatitudes. They are represented as a Queen wearing a crown and holding a sceptre in one hand and bearing a shield carrying symbols on a coat of arms in the other. In the case of Concord and Friendship the shield bears two pairs of outward facing doves. Another example in the cathedral of Auxerre, shows a female figure holding a disc with a dove representing Humility, which is seen alongside a rider being thrown from his horse, the symbol of Pride.

Prudence, as one of the four cardinal virtues, carried the meaning of wisdom as wise conduct rather than mere caution and together with humility has been assumed to be based on the words in the gospel of Matthew; "Be ye therefore wise as serpents, and harmless as doves" (*Matthew* 10: 16). However, more distant links with the serpent and dove symbols of the Mother Goddess may have been an influence, more particularly in old testament references to wisdom in the book of *Proverbs*. Centuries later wisdom alone was extolled in a 17th-century book of emblems: "Man's life no temper more doth bless than simple prudent harmlessness" (George Wither). From the Renaissance onwards, the two virtues were often combined allegorically in one work as can be seen in paintings such as the portrait of *Venetia Stanley, Lady Digby* after van Dyck, depicted as Prudence, and an even earlier variation on the theme but also incorporating doves and snakes entitled *An Allegory of Innocence and Guile* by the 16th-century artist Maerten van Heemskerck which includes a very life-like dove in flight. The painting of *Prudentia* by Vittore Carpaccio was probably painted

(*below left*) An Allegory of Innocence and Guile *showing a very life-like dove in flight, by the 16th-century Maerten van Heemskerck.* (*by kind permission of The Bowes Museum, Barnard Castle, Durham*)

(*below right*) Prudentia *by Vittore Carpaccio (1460-1526), with mirror, dove and dragon.* (*High Museum of Art, Atlanta, Georgia, Gift of the Samuel H. Kress Foundation, 58.36*)

c.1492-1500 and may be a fragment of a larger work. She holds a mirror in one hand and a staff in the other. A dove perches on a low branch, just above a very fearsome-looking dragon. In a depiction of the Presentation of the Virgin, now in the Uffizi Gallery, Florence, she appears as a spectator next to the kneeling figure of the Virgin.

117

In the late Middle Ages a mirror was often included in scenes showing these two virtues; it was believed to have signified that the wise man has the ability to see himself as he really is. This emblematic connection may perhaps have echoed much earlier origins, as exemplified by an ancient cylinder seal on which the winged goddess holds a mirror in each hand and a later Etruscan scene on the back of a mirror showing the Greek goddess Leda with her swan, together with the goddess Astarte and her dove, and holding a mirror in one hand.

A popular allegory known as *The Ladder of Virtue* was based on Jacob's dream in the Old Testament, in which angels ascend and descend between heaven and earth. It was originally directed towards those in holy orders as an exhortation to leave worldliness behind and achieve the virtues of Faith, Hope and Charity in the form of Christ at the summit. In several manuscripts, allegorical figures personifying helpful virtues or hindering vices appear on the ladder or alongside, either encouraging or impeding the ascent. The 12th-century Benedictine abbess, Hildegard of Bingen, was a celebrated mystic and writer who experienced apocalyptic visions and in her book *Scivias*, she describes in words and vivid illuminations the subject of Creation, Redemption and Salvation. She reflects the iconographic convention of the period but adds her own interpretations, some of which are so bizarre that it has been suggested that the distorting premonitory symptoms of migraine, from which she is known to have suffered, might have been responsible. In her portrayal of the Ladder of Virtue, the dove appears towards the foot, hovering just above Chastity, who is holding the figure of a boy symbolising innocence. Another

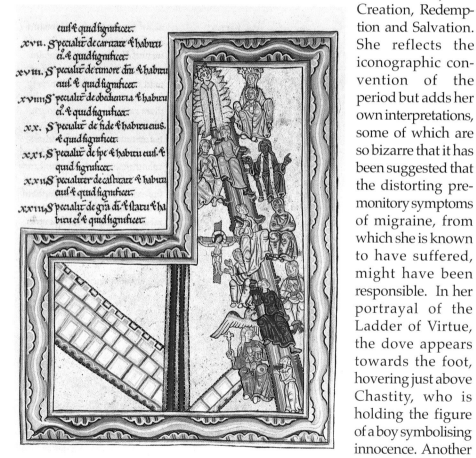

The Ladder of Virtue, with a dove appearing at the bottom, hovering above the figure of Chastity. (Abbey of St Hildegard, Rüdesheim, Germany)

vision is entitled The Column of Divine Words which bears an image of the dove on its summit. In branches springing from the side, there are figures of Abraham, Moses and Joshua, together with other patriarchs and prophets, while on another aspect, apostles, martyrs, confessors and young females are grouped. The text describes a dove carrying in its beak a ray of golden light and this feature is also applied to the crescent moon motif carried by the blue and white dove surmounting the summit.

During the Renaissance there was a secularising movement in moral allegory in which artists made increasing use of deities and classical mythology, also the heroes and heroines of ancient history, especially Roman, to personify moral qualities. The 16th century was a period of great activity for humanist compilers of handbooks of mythography who drew on antique and medieval sources, adding their own, often fanciful, explanations of the emblems they were presenting. An important factor among the ancient Greeks was their belief that Egyptian hieroglyphics were symbolic images in which esoteric information was concealed. Early in the 15th century a Florentine priest brought back from the island of Andros a manuscript written in the 5th century by an Alexandrian named Horapollo Niliacus, which appeared to support this view. This work, known as the *Hieroglyphica*, together with the Christian *Physiologus*, linked the lives of animals and man allegorically and represented a fusion of the classical tradition with oriental antique art and religion. Horapollo's book was also one reason for the great revival of interest in the language of symbols and in things Egyptian generally at the time. Included in it, for example, the lion signified strength; the serpent represented eternity, but with its tail in its mouth it stood for the universe; and rebellious sons were symbolised by the hippopotamus, which was an Egyptian symbol of fertility. In this work the dove was also featured in several rather irrational ways. In a story of man's ingratitude the dove is claimed to desert its cohort in order to mate with its mother, but in a different context it was also recommended as a food to protect against epidemics. Finally, a black dove was said to symbolise a woman who remained a widow until death, because the hen bird was believed, probably inaccurately, to do the same.

Another early handbook to appear was by Andreas Alciati in 1531, consisting of illustrations with hidden symbolic meanings, together with a verse explaining the underlying moral, reminiscent of Aesop's Fables. Naked Venus, standing with one foot on a tortoise flanked by two doves on the ground, teaches that woman's place is in the home and that she should know when to hold her tongue.

A scholarly and influential work entitled *Iconologia* by Cesare Ripa, published in 1593, was not only a dictionary of virtues and vices, but also contained broader entries such as Abundance, Pure Air, Sincerity and Zeal, which represented a rather wider scope than the original seven virtues. It drew on many sources including classical authors, the Bible, the bestiary and borrowings from other authors and often featured the female figure, as in the *Psychomachia*. In the

A black dove, with diverse symbolic meaning, from the 15th century. (Barbara Frears, from Horapollo, Les Sculptures ou Gravures Sacrées d'Orus Apollo, *1553)*

Naked Venus with her foot on a tortoise, a dove on either side. (Barbara Frears from Andreas Alciati, Emblematum Liber, *1531)*

119

Wisdom or Sapienza portrayed as the Roman Goddess Minerva but holding the dove as the Holy Spirit and the lamb in her other hand; from a 17th-century work on virtues and vices.
(*from* Iconologia di Cesare Ripa Perugino, *1630 edition*)

The dove symbolising Sincerity.
(*from* Iconologia di Cesare Ripa Perugino, *1709 edition*)

1630 edition, Sapienza Divina is portrayed as the Roman goddess Athene (Minerva) with a cock on her helmet and holding a white dove as the Holy Ghost in one hand and a book with the Christian lamb symbol upon it in the other. The book's seven hanging pendants may indicate the seven gifts of the spirit or the seven sacraments. Sapienza or Wisdom was sometimes interpreted as the cardinal virtue Prudence, although the latter was judged to be a lesser virtue; "How much better is it to get wisdom than gold! and to get understanding rather to be chosen than silver!" (*Proverbs* 16: 16). Also included in Ripa's work is a female figure representing Sincerity, who holds a white dove in one hand and a heart in the other, while in a later edition we find the cardinal virtues of Divine Justice represented by a crowned goddess holding a sword in one hand and a pair of scales in the other, with a dove flying overhead. Also in this edition, Pure Air is shown as a female figure holding a white dove in one hand and a banner in the other, while a zephyr or breeze from a cloud blows upon her.

In Gabriel Rollenhagen's work *Nucleus Emblematum Selectissimorum*, compiled in 1611, one engraving which the author calls "Wise Innocence" shows a pair of confronting serpents twined around a staff surmounted by a dove. Nowadays this emblem is widely recognised as the *Caduceus*, the traditional and enduring symbol of medicine. However, a single serpent around a staff originally represented the Greek god Asklepios (Aesculapius) and was an early symbol of healing. The double version belonged to the god Hermes (Mercury) who later became a central figure in Alchemy. Among his several influences he was

*The Caduceus emblem by Hans
Holbein the Younger, 1523,
incorporated into a printer's device.
(Oeffentliche Kunstsammlung
Basel, Kunstmuseum, Switzerland,
photograph by Martin Bühler)*

credited with curative powers which helps to explain how his symbol entered
medicine by way of alchemical chemistry and pharmacy. The appearance of
the dove or occasionally a pair of wings on the staff may have either been linked
with Mercury as the winged messenger or been based on the scriptural link of
the snake and dove as symbols of wisdom and meekness.

The work *Symbolorum et Emblematum* (1654) by Ioachimo Camerario follows the pattern of combining classical and Christian interpretations of the accompanying images. In describing the dove as messenger of divine peace, a section of the text elaborates upon Pliny's description of the bird as a useful emissary in war and then switches to the Old Testament story of Noah and the Flood and finally describes the Christian allegory called 'Inside and Out'. This compares the dove, which is alleged to be without bile (fault) and displays a white exterior to those with true piety and simplicity who must ensure that their words and deeds match correspondingly. A more straightforward Christian interpretation of a classical tale subtitled 'Whence the gleam of gold shone through the branches' recounts the legend of Aeneas in which two doves sent by his mother Venus lead him to the tree on which a golden branch grows. This is said to symbolise Wisdom, which in Christianity is interpreted as God's help to understanding by guided action and acquisition of knowledge.

ALCHEMY

The roots of Alchemy date back to the 4th century BC philosophers, Plato and Aristotle. They borrowed some of their knowledge from Egyptian priests who were known to have sought a medicine that would lead to immortality. Other influences were adopted over the centuries from the Persians, Jews, Christians and Muslims to produce an arcane system based on chemistry and philosophy, which flourished in the Middle Ages and became known as the Hermetic Art. The main aim of the alchemists was to discover the secret of the mystical 'philosopher's stone', once described as

> the stone which is not a stone; a precious thing which has no value; a thing of many shapes, which has no shape; this unknown, which is known to all.

In spite of this cryptic description, the alchemists believed that it would not only transmute base metals or the four elements – air, fire, water and earth – into gold or silver, but was also capable of regenerating and prolonging life. Many believed that its true aim was actually philosophical in nature and was directed at developing inner enlightenment and spiritual transformation, which has recently been described as a divine spark which can become a candle to illuminate the whole inner self. In this belief it resembled several early sects such as the Gnostics.

The basis of alchemical practice stemmed from the view that the whole of reality had been created from the non-physical *materia prima*, sometimes represented as the dragon or serpent, *serpens mercurii* or base matter, which was said to create and destroy itself. The dove symbolised the soul hidden in this matter and, together with the eagle, another elemental sky-heaven symbol, epitomised the liberated spirit. In the symbolic transformation of the *materia prima*, also called the Great Work or *magnum opus*, sometimes symbolised by the moon conjoined with the sun, several chemical reactions were involved. The chief element, the philosophical sulphur, was said to equate symbolically to the male, red, solar and hot principles, while mercury represented white, female, lunar and cold energy. Together these passed through several stages and in one allegorical equation reappeared as the Red King known as Sulphur of the Wise together with the White Queen called Mercury or the Red Rose. Finally, the king and queen became united in the fire of love known as the sacred marriage and from their union perfection was said to emerge. This was claimed to represent the philosopher's stone, the catalyst capable of transforming base metals into gold and the key to spiritual enlightenment.

A dove descending on the alchemical King and Queen bathing in the aqua permanens *of Mercury. (from a series of 20 woodcuts in* Rosarium Philosophorum, *published in Frankfurt in 1550)*

In pursuit of their aims, the alchemists toiled away with their crucibles, retorts and furnaces, with the result that many of them became sensible and practical chemists in later centuries, but the philosophical and mystical elements of their beliefs tended to predominate from an early stage. One of their most important tools was the symbolic hermetic vessel, the *vas hermetis*, in which the Great Work of transformation, often accompanied by the flight of a dove either upwards or downwards, took place. The process was believed to hold the key to all mysteries and to contain powers of physical and spiritual healing. Reference to the process being "matured by wisdom and artificial fire" and another to the "shining white dove, called the salt of metals, being hidden in the lead of the philosophers, to be liberated as symbol of the guiding spirit", reveals the strange combination of what today seems to be incompatible and incongruous ideas. An unusual example appears in a 16th-century German tract on the philosopher's stone in which a naked conjugal couple seek the blessing of the Holy Spirit symbolised by the dove:

> The red man here to his white wife
> is maryed with the spryte of life.

(above) *Two symbolic hermetic vessels:*
(top) *The dove is shown flying towards the sun and the moon conjoined, symbolising the great work.*
(bottom) *The dove rises from the base matter, below which is the frog-like* Physis *representing the sensual nature of man and emitting the four elements – fire, air, water and earth. (Barbara Frears from Johann Barchusen,* Elementa Chemiae, *1718)*

A naked conjugal couple inside a hermetic vessel invoking the blessing of the dove as Holy Spirit. Physis *signifies man's carnal nature and the serpent symbolises the base matter. (by permission of* The British Library, *Ms Egerton 845, fol.15, 16)*

Hermes inside the hermetic vessel, supported by angels, with the sun and the moon, and doves below, some carrying branches. (Barbara Frears from Mutus Liber, *17th century)*

The alchemists adopted the god Hermes (Mercury) in the early days and endowed him with their own allegorical meanings as well as using his traditional role as winged messenger of the gods. He was sometimes called the triple-natured Hermes in the form of three living things, king, queen and dove, and as the Hermes bird he symbolised the divine spirit that would be liberated after union had been accomplished. He was also referred to as the secret transforming subject, the divine spirit dwelling in all creatures and one of his synonyms was the *aqua permanens*. In a 17th-century pictorial book the philosopher's stone is shown being heated in the alchemist's furnace, while Mercury wearing his winged helmet is shown above within the hermetic vessel, supported by angels. The sun shines overhead and two of several doves bearing branches in their beaks fly below. This image emphasised that the physical operation of alchemy in the furnace below mirrored the spiritual reality above.

125

Lux nox – a dove over the face of the waters in the story of the Creation, combined with the separation of light from darkness. (Barbara Frears)

Hermes Trismegistus, which meant thrice-greatest Hermes, was the name given to a central figure in alchemy who was claimed to be the author of certain books of mysticism and alchemy. He was founded on a semi-legendary Egyptian sage whom the alchemists identified with Thoth, the great Egyptian god of wisdom and intelligence. In a book by Robert Flood of Chester, published in 1617, the author alludes to Hermes Trismegistus and, like other early writers, describes the dove in various symbolic guises. These include the Holy Spirit; the Soul of the World; God's Fiery Spirit; and the Light of the World which is carried over the face of the waters, the latter no doubt being an allusion to the Creation story in the book of *Genesis*. Nowadays many might prefer the more prosaic interpretation of Roger Scruton writing in *England: an Elegy* (2000) in which he compares the dove or Holy Ghost with English common law – always present, always vigilant, always personal and always benign. In one of Flood's accompanying engravings the dove is dramatically illustrated

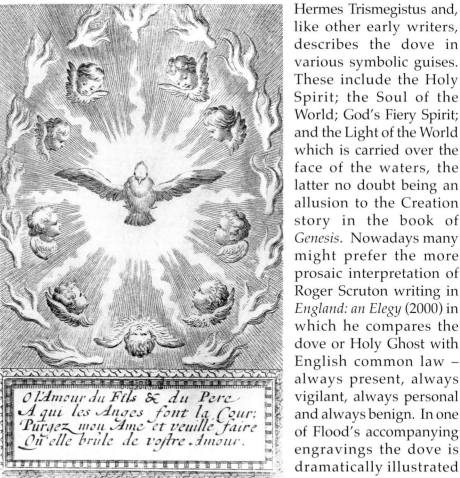

A 17th-century engraving by Abraham Bosse of a dove in an aureole with heads of winged amoretti and flames around. (cliché Bibliothèque Nationale de France)

emanating from heaven in a swirl of light. Another work of the same period by Abraham Bosse shows the bird in flight surrounded by rays of light, winged cherubs and flames of fire.

An alchemical treatise of the late 16th century, known as *Splendours of the Sun*, became famous for its magnificent illuminated depictions of the *magnum opus* and is now held as an unique manuscript on vellum in the British Library. Very little is known about its author, Salomon Trismosin, but in more recent times it is thought that he might have been a fictitious character. Included amongst its allegorical pictures (see next page) is one set in the courtyard of a magnificent palace, in which a naked, bearded man with a white dove on his head, is shown immersed breast-high in a cauldron of water. A second man fans the furnace with bellows. The interpretation of this obscure scene is that the central figure, sometimes identified as Mercury, is undergoing regeneration in the *aqua permanens*, the dove above his head in a halo of light representing the liberated divine spirit. The flask on the step further symbolises the alchemical rejuvenation process.

Another scene from *Splendours of the Sun* depicts a courtyard in which a large central alchemical vessel contains three fighting doves, red, white and black, the latter being under attack by the other two (see page 129). Are these colours an allusion to the early mythological symbolism of the ancient goddess in which white represented the new moon and the goddess as a maiden; red stood for the harvest moon and the goddess as a nymph; and black symbolised her as the waning moon and the old crone? Around this central feature are several vignettes combining Christian and earlier sources, including one scene which depicts the Pope crowning a kneeling figure. At the top is an enigmatic picture of a chariot drawn by two peacocks; the rider is holding two arrows while a helmeted figure kneels before him.

Many early alchemists were devout Christians who chose to seek knowledge through direct experience rather than by blind faith. Men such as Thomas Aquinas and Isaac Newton considered the study of alchemy to be a complement to established religion and philosophy rather than a substitute. Illustrations in some later alchemical treatises show the participants being handed down secrets of the cult from God in heaven, while others portray the dove and Lamb of God, together with Mercury and other arcane alchemical allusions. In the 17th century, with the coming of modern chemistry, the alchemist had more or less lost his standing and had tended to become an object of derision. At the end of the 19th century, Carl Jung, who was making a psychological study of the subject, in particular as an interpretation of the collective unconscious, was driven to remark: "The diversity of symbolic material means that it is difficult to perceive any order at all". However, this did not stop him from expounding his own views of the deeper archetypal meanings which he found within the subject.

Hermes as an old man undergoing a rejuvenation process in the Bath of Fire. The dove and the hermetic vessel are linked with the procedure. The surrounding border contains a bee, a butterfly and a wealth of birds among the beautifully depicted wild flowers. From the 16th-century alchemical treatise Splendours of the Sun. *(by permission of The British Library, Ms Harley 3469, fol.21)*

Another scene from Splendours of the Sun depicts an elaborate courtyard with a large central alchemical vessel containing three fighting doves, while surrounding scenes combine Christian and mythological sources.
(by permission of The British Library, Ms Harley 3469, fol.24)

129

MESSENGERS & SPORT

The role of the pigeon as messenger must have been recognised very early. Noah was familiar with it and an early record, dating from 2500 BC, comes from Sumer, an ancient city lying between the Tigris and Euphrates. In a text commemorating the victory of the city over its trespassing neighbours, the ruler dispatched two pigeons to carry news to the sanctuaries of the gods in their cities. Much later, in the 5th century BC, it is believed that Cyrus the Great established a network of pigeon messengers in Assyria and Persia, while the existence of a similar flying network connecting the important centres on the coasts of the eastern Mediterranean, possibly dating from Phoenician times or earlier, was propounded by Charles Sibillot. He named one of the chief sites as Paphos in Cyprus, where an important temple of the Great Goddess, together with a dovecote, was maintained. Writing recently, Josip Pekanovic refers to the pigeon mail, which once connected Egypt with cities as far north as Baghdad during the reign of Sultan Nur-ed-din, in 1146. He built pigeon lofts in Cairo and Damascus and used the birds extensively for carrying messages concerning administration, diplomacy, trade and war.

(above) Early pigeon mail in the Near East.
(Josip Pekanovic)

Sailors on the high seas in antiquity used to release birds from their ships in order to detect from their flight the proximity of land. Votive boats from the Bronze Age in Sardinia having dove images on board may support this idea, while Indian fables of the 6th century BC related that Indian sailors used the flight of birds from their ships rather than navigating by the stars, later confirmed by the Roman writer Pliny (AD 23-79). The suitability of the pigeon by comparison with the raven lay in that bird's inherent homing instinct, which could be depended upon even when it was sent off from an unfamiliar environment. The Old Testament story of Noah and the Deluge combines the usefulness of both birds; the raven sent out first from the Ark in order to steer for land, to be followed later by the dove to ascertain the chances of landing on it.

(right) Boat-shaped bronze lamp, with a dove perched on the suspension ring, from Sardinia, c.900-800 BC.
(Irit Ziffer)

130

One of the most important attributes of the ancient mother goddess was her power of delivering oracles. As temple birds, the pigeon's instinct to return to the nest from considerable distances must have been recognised and exploited in earliest times. Several references in Assyrian and Babylonian writings, dating from the second millennium BC attest to the pigeon's use in this way, for example, "divination by means of a dove" and "a ritual for the evil portended by a dove". Among the oracular shrines in Greece the most ancient was at Dodona in Epirus, which was dedicated originally to the woodland goddess Dione and later to Zeus (Jupiter). Legend relates that the cooings and flight patterns of the doves perched on oak trees there were observed and interpreted as signs and portents.

Bernard de Montfaucon, writing in 1719, describes the unusual Roman image of a dove standing on a ram's head as being "most curious and extraordinary" and enlarges upon the ancient Greek legend, originally told by the Greek historian Herodotus, writing in the 5th century BC, in which two doves flew from Thebes in Upper Egypt. One, sometimes said to be black, flew to Dodona, where it delivered oracles, while the other went to Libya, where it settled on a ram's head between its horns. In quoting classical writers, Montfaucon repeats the allegorical fancy that the horns represented the ears and the head of Zeus. When the Egyptian god Amun (Ammon) became identified with Zeus, he acquired the ram as an attribute.

The Etruscans are believed to have used messenger pigeons as part of a forecasting service for fishermen. It was probably similar to the coastal stations in the Mediterranean described by Strabo (63 BC-AD 21) as "places for watching tunny fish". The pigeons were trained to fly between lookout points to carry news of the arrival of tunny fish shoals to nearby fishermen along the coast. The interesting Etruscan wall painting, which was found in the tomb of hunting and fishing at Corneto (Tarquinia), dating from 500 BC, is generally interpreted as a scene combining fishing at sea with the figure of a man on land aiming sling-shot at the birds in sight. However, another possibility is that the birds, probably pigeons, are being released from one coastal fishing station to fly along the coast to another with news of the shoals. The contraption may have been a type of leather castanet which made whip-like noises to urge them on their way.

Early Greek coin showing doves in the trees at the oracle of Zeus in Dodona. (Barbara Frears from A.O. Cook, Zeus, God of the Bright Sky, *1914)*

(above) Roman image of a ram's head stopper with dove on top. (Barbara Frears, from Laurentius Beger, Gemmarum et Numismatum Graecorum, *1696)*

(left) Tunny fishing in an Etruscan wall-painting, now in the British Museum. (Barbara Frears from Charles Sibillot, Lo Sport colombofilo negli antichi tempi, *1920)*

Cypriot coin of the Roman Empire showing a pair of rooftop doves and fish in the forecourt pool.
(Barbara Frears from Jean Lajard, Recherches sue le Culte, les symboles, les attributs, et les monuments figurés de Vénus ..., 1837)

Away from the realms of myth and legend the Greeks and Romans seem to have known the tame pigeon very well and to have made a hobby of breeding fancy varieties as well as using them as messengers. Pliny, writing in the 1st century, said: "Many people have quite a mania for pigeons, building turrets for them on house roofs and tracing the pedigree of single birds." Also in Roman times, Ovid, writing at the beginning of the Christian era, described a pigeon, dyed purple for easy identification, being sent home by a youth with news of his success at the Olympic Games. Half a century or so earlier, Varro wrote about the ladies who were in the habit of taking tame pigeons to the amphitheatre where they "let them loose from their bosoms" during the spectacle to fly home ahead. Was this merely a diversion, or were they taking back some domestic message?

A traditional aspect of the Olympic Games was the liberation of a flight of white doves during the opening ceremony which originally symbolised the sacred armistice prohibiting all warfare during the month of the festival. A tragic accident in Seoul in 1988 during the evening ceremony, when birds flew up into the Olympic flame and were burnt to death, put an end to this tradition. In subsequent years, however, symbolic traces of the custom have survived including an attractive parade of young people carrying fluttering dove models on poles around the arena. At the Sydney games in 2000, the image of a large white dove carrying an olive branch in its beak was projected onto an immense white sheet covering the teams in the stadium. At the headquarters of the International Olympic Committee in Lausanne, the Peace Statue of a goddess holding a white dove in her hand was made in 1987, copied from the original sculpture made in Greece in 450 BC.

Image of a dove with an olive branch, projected over the heads of the teams in the arena during the opening ceremony of the Olympic Games at Sydney, 2000.
(I.O.C./Olympic Museum Collection, Lausanne, Switzerland)

In England, peaceful use of the birds as messengers seems to have arrived relatively late, although trained homing pigeons were brought to Europe from Persia in the 16th century and, long before that, returning Crusaders must have been familiar with the custom in the Near East. Thomas Fuller, writing in 1662 suggested that English pigeons might be used for the purpose. He referred to the pigeon-post in the East, but added the warning that adoption of the messenger birds might put the postmen out of work. However, this proposal does not seem to have been carried out as a century or so later John Moore gives the impression that the birds were still an exciting novelty rather than an established custom. It was until the 19th century that a pigeon-post became established in Europe. The birds were quicker than the mail-coaches and provided a valuable adjunct to other means of communication. When Baron Reuter started his well-known organisation for collecting and transmitting news on the Continent he employed pigeons, not only in addition to telegraphy, but also to fill missing gaps in the railway networks, particularly between Berlin and Paris.

Sending a message by Pigeon Post. (Richard Blake)

The Peace Statue by Stavros Georgopoulos at the headquarters of the International Olympic Committee, Lausanne, copied from a Greek sculpture of 450 BC. (I.O.C./Olympic Museum Collection, Lausanne, Switzerland)

133

(above) Coat of arms of the College of Heralds in London. (photograph by Peter Hansell)

(below) Messenger pigeons on a woodcut from a 17th-century edition of Sir John Mandeville's travels.

Among the several duties of heralds in early times in England was that of making state or royal proclamations; of carrying messages between princes or sovereign powers and also of arranging public processions, funerals and state ceremonials. In addition, they became involved in settling names and pedigrees of those entitled to armorial bearings. The College of Heralds which was established in 1484 now occupies a 17th-century building in London and is fronted by a magnificent wrought-iron gate of a later date bearing the arms of the College. This carries a shield on which the red cross of St George encloses four blue pigeons with red legs, above which is a crest-coronet carrying a single blue bird with raised wings. The dove or pigeon as messenger had become the traditional symbol of the heralds at an early date and a painting of Henry VIII's time has the words 'secret' and 'diligent' written beside the open and closed wings of the bird. In another heraldic context, the head of a blue dove wearing a gold coronet surmounts the white staves customarily carried by heralds at the time of their installation. Among the clergy, the dove carrying an olive branch in its beak as the traditional symbol of peace and reconciliation is often featured on the arms of bishops. A few modern examples include the dove which flies overhead carrying a declaration of the nation's independence on the arms of Liberia and the bird in the arms of the Republic of Cyprus which became independent in 1960, which may represent the hoped-for peace between the Greeks and Turks on the island.

The record of pigeons as wartime messengers over the centuries is a moving and little-known epic. Scattered references describe the many acts of bravery performed by these valiant birds. They were used in Roman times during the siege of Modena; in the Crusades; in the days of the great Mughal emperor Akbar; and during the siege of Paris in 1870-71. In the Near East the custom was well described by the 14th-century English traveller, Sir John Mandeville, whose writings were often fabricated and based on the travels of others, though this account seems plausible:

> The people of these countries have a strange custom in time of war and siege; when they dare not send out messengers with letters to ask for help, they write their letters and tie them to the neck of a colver and let the colver fly away. They immediately seek the place where they have been brought up and nourished and are at once relieved of their messages by their owners and desired aid is sent to the besieged.
> (*The Voiage and Travaile of Sir John Maundevile*, 1356)

The attachment of messages around the neck is evident in some woodcuts, but other positions such as the wing, leg and tail-feathers were also used. However, the likelihood of birds carrying letters in their beaks seems a trifle far-fetched

and probably owes more to artistic licence than reality. Some centuries later, in 1845, five years after the appearance in Great Britain of the very first postage stamp, the city-state of Basle brought out its own stamps, which included the well-known Basle Dove. This original stamp was intended to advertise the dove as a means for rapid transmission of written messages and features a white carrier-pigeon in bold relief bearing a letter in its beak. The stamp was reproduced in 1995 on miniature sheets to commemorate the 150th anniversary of its creation.

(above) Pigeons carrying sealed messages in their beaks in a 15th-century German woodcut. (Colin Osman)

(left) The Basle Dove in the 1995 commemorative sheet. (Dr. Daniel Haag-Wackernagel)

(below) A variety of postage stamps showing the Blue Rock Pigeon, Columba livia, some with dovecote or nesting boxes.

135

(above) Mobile pigeon loft used behind the trenches in World War I. (Royal Signals Museum, Blandford)

(right) A pigeon parachute used on the Western Front in World War I. (Barbara Frears from a photograph by Peter Hansell)

(below) Pigeon wearing a camera on its breast for aerial recording. (© Stefan Richter)

In Britain it is estimated that pigeon breeders gave 100,000 birds to the war effort at the outbreak of the First World War. Members of the crews of tanks, seaplanes and submarines were trained to handle the homing pigeons that they carried. They were also kept in mobile lofts behind the trenches on the front lines in Europe and often had to fly through gun barrages and clouds of poison gas in order to deliver their messages to base. Speaking of the military value of the homing pigeon, Major-General Fowler, Chief of the Department of Signals and Communications of the British Army said:

> It is the pigeon on which we must and do depend when every other method fails. During quiet periods we can rely on telephone, telegraph, flag signals, our dogs and various other ways in use on the front with the British Army, but when the battle rages and everything gives way to barrage and machine-gun fire, to say nothing of gas attacks and bombing, it is to the pigeon that we go for succour. When troops are lost or surrounded in the mazes on the front, or are advancing and yet beyond the known localities, then we depend absolutely on the pigeon for our communications. Regular methods in such cases are worthless and it is at just such times that we need most messengers that we can rely on. In the pigeons we have them. I am glad to say that they have never failed us.

Improved telecommunication during the Second World War reduced the need for pigeon messengers to some extent. Nevertheless, thousands of birds were given to the National Pigeon Service by British breeders at the outbreak of war. They were used not only in Europe, but as far afield as India and Burma and in the USA large numbers of Racing homers were donated to the American Pigeon Corps. In Britain the birds were employed in the Intelligence Service as in the First World War and often accom-panied agents when dropped by parachute. Invaluable details from these missions were relayed back about German V1 and V2 rocket sites on the other side of the Channel and strategic information was also gathered in the months preceding the Allied landings on D-Day. The birds were carried routinely on bomber planes and were particularly useful in sea-rescue emergencies.

An intriguing wartime aspect of pigeons was their use in recording aerial photographic images for strategic purposes by means of a specially designed, self-operating, miniature camera mounted on a canvas breast harness.

Man's debt to the pigeons' heroism has been recognised by civic memorials and individual awards in both World Wars, but no doubt many birds died unknown and unrecorded. Among several impressive edifices commemorating these losses on both sides of the conflict are those at Lille, France, Berlin-Spandau and at Quai aux Barques in Brussels. In this country there is no monument on such a scale, but at the animal cemetery of the Peoples' Dispensary for Sick Animals at Ilford an individual headstone marks the grave of 'Mary of Exeter' who played her part in the First World War. Another modest memorial to these "warrior birds" in a municipal park at Worthing, Sussex, has unfortunately been repeatedly vandalised. At the beginning of this millennium it is appropriate and welcome to learn of a proposal to erect a new memorial in London dedicated to all creatures, including pigeons, that suffered or died in both World Wars.

(below left) The memorial in Brussels to pigeons lost in war, with a 'helmet' symbol on a pillar, supported by birds.
(Barbara Frears from a photograph by Nicholas Philpot)

(below right) The Berlin-Spandau memorial to messenger pigeons lost in World War I.
(Barbara Frears from a photograph by Peter Hansell)

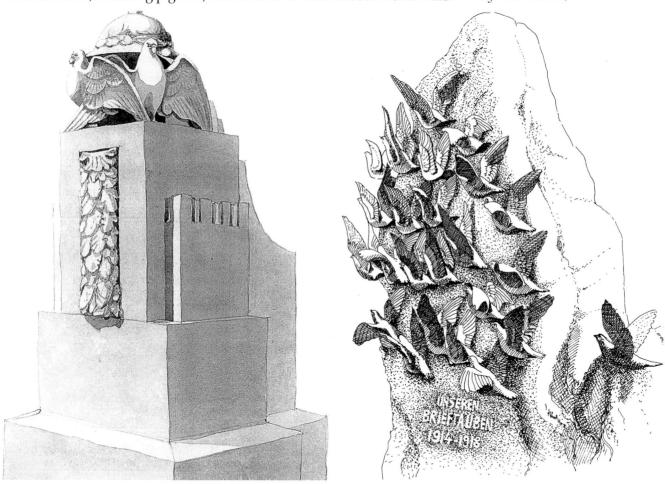

In China the release of pigeons carrying little flutes or whistles is a custom believed to date from the 12th century. These devices, weighing only a few grams, are still made today from bamboo, gourds, lightweight wood and,

Chinese pigeon whistles made from bamboo and gourds.
(photograph by Peter Hansell)

more recently, plastic. They are commonly fitted in an upright position to the middle tail feathers near the rump. The whistles make musical sounds in flight, which have been described by the Chinese as 'heavenly music' or voices of the spirits of their ancestors. Early western observers concluded that the object of their use was mainly to scare away hawks and other predators of the birds in flight, but more recently it has emerged that the custom was primarily intended for aesthetic pleasure. A latter-day Chinese enthusiast owned 300 different whistles, which were combined to play celestial music when attached in turn to his 20 flying birds. The custom is also practised in Indonesia, Taiwan and Bali and many pigeon whistles find their way across the Pacific to Australia where they have become collector's

Chinese whistle made from a gourd and attached to a pigeon. The whistle plays several notes. (Pitt-Rivers Museum, University of Oxford)

pieces. A fine collection was recently amassed by the late Dr Hannaford Schafer of Melbourne. These are beautifully crafted and include one unusual flute in the shape of a pig's head; also several gourds, beautifully lacquered, in which a series of tuned bamboo cylindrical whistles are inserted around the periphery. A similar collection of polyphonous whistles, originally from Beijing and Shanghai, is to be found at the Pitt-Rivers Museum in Oxford.

The ancient sport of *Triganieri* has been followed for centuries in many parts of the world such as Italy, Spain, Egypt, India and Persia. The pursuit exploited the pigeon's tendency to fly together in flocks in the sky and, with training, to entice other pigeons back into its own loft. In action, a flight or 'kit' was released into the sky simultaneously with birds from nearby, usually rooftop, lofts. After mingling together, the birds were signalled down by their owners with flags or whistles and were rewarded with titbits, any strange birds meanwhile being taken captive. Contests generally took place on a friendly basis, but they could be fiercely competitive and even result in ransom or slaughter of the captured birds. The survival of an illustrated 18th-century Arab treatise written by Sayid Muhammad Valih Musavi, which describes various aspects of pigeon keeping, also includes the scene of a rooftop frame for birds together with the pigeon keeper carrying his stave (see also next two pages). In the early days in northern Italy, the bird known as the Modena was used under the name of Triganica from which the sport gets its name. This original bird had a much slimmer build than its modern counterpart of which many chubbier and more colourful varieties are now bred.

Rooftop Persian birds with their keeper. These were possibly used for the sport of Triganieri.
(by permission of The British Library, Ms IO Persian 4811, fol.4)

139

Persian pigeon-keeping, from an
18th-century Arab treatise by Sayid
Muhammad Valih Musavi. Note the
ground-floor pigeon cote.
(by permission of The British Library,
Ms IO Persian 4811, fol.5)

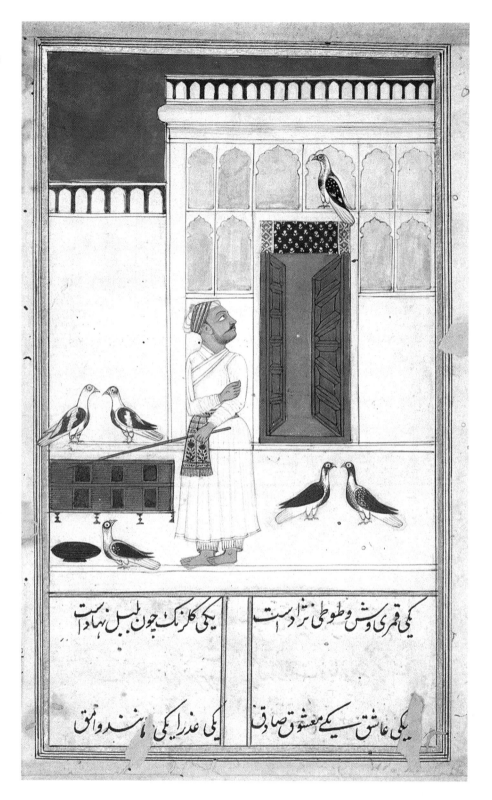

A crowded scene of domestic pigeons, again from Musavi's treatise. The birds are shown in outdoor ground-floor cotes and some in an indoor cage.
(by permission of The British Library, Ms IO Persian 4811, fol.1)

The present-day pastime of pigeon racing may have originated in the ancient custom of using the birds as messengers. In Europe, however, one important stimulus was the success of the specially-trained homing pigeons, which were used to deliver mail from outside the city during the Siege of Paris in the Franco-Prussian War (1870-71). This not only popularised the sport, but also led to the establishment of military pigeon stations in Europe at the end of that century. The breeding of the modern racing pigeon, or homer, in the west took place partly in Britain and the USA, but mainly in Belgium where it has been the national sport for more than a century.

A Pigeon Fancier, an early example of naïve art by an unknown artist. (The Portal Gallery, London, photograph by Adrian Hansell)

Today's racing pigeon fancier is often a combination of owner, breeder, trainer and punter. The buying and selling of the pick of these highly-bred birds is carried out on an international scale and current champions fetch phenomenal prices. Races are controlled by local clubs, which supervise timing of the birds with special tamper-proof clocks and, latterly, with electronic timing devices.

As well as racing pigeon enthusiasts there are also large numbers of breeders of fancy birds in many parts of the world. The innumerable varieties of these domestic fancy pigeons which exist today are all descended from one single species, the Blue Rock Pigeon (*Columba livia*). Selective breeding

Racing Pigeons by E.H. Windred, 1922, oil on canvas. Paintings like this were given as prizes to winning owners of racing birds up until the Second World War.
(purchased by the Peter Moores Foundation for display at Compton Verney, Warwickshire, © Compton Verney, photograph by Hugh Kelly)

143

by fanciers took place very early, chiefly in the Middle East, but also in India and the Orient, and was carried out in Europe from the 16th century onwards. It is not surprising that the astonishing variety and individual beauty of the many breeds has captured the imagination of artists throughout the ages.

Pigeon-shooting matches became popular in England towards the end of the 18th century. Several clubs were established for pigeon shoots, including the Hurlingham Club in 1869 which became a popular venue, particularly among the aristocracy. The pigeon's welfare was ostensibly protected by the London Gun Club but in spite of this the sport aroused considerable antagonism and a ban was finally imposed in 1905. Clay-pigeon or trap shooting was subsequently introduced in which various 'shooting targets' and mechanisms for launching them were developed. This later became a sport in its own right.

The Dove Shooters, *a painting by the Hungarian artist Tamas Galambos, from 1978. (Magyar Nemzeti Galeria, Budapest, Hungary/Bridgeman Art Library)*

144

A Blue Pouter Cock.
(photograph by Peter Hansell from
Robert Fulton, The Illustrated
Book of Pigeons, *1874)*

Varieties of Fancy Pigeon.
(Author's collection)

MODERN IMAGES: 1845-2000

The movement known as the Pre-Raphaelite Brotherhood was founded in 1845 by the artists Dante Gabriel Rossetti, John Everett Millais and William Holman Hunt. In the early days, fired by the enthusiasm of youth, their style was inspired by predominantly medieval subjects; the use of intense colour; and the need for a close study of nature. An underlying aim was to restore to British art the freshness and conviction that had been found in painting before the era of Raphael. They were initially subject to considerable criticism and this was sometimes coupled with accusations of Romish tendencies, but John Ruskin was an early supporter and defender of their views. He highlighted in particular the prophetic role of the artist, suggesting that it could be as influential as the Church as a vehicle for idealism.

In religious subjects, the artists sought to create new interpretations that would replace the traditional iconography, thus reviving the language of symbolism and typology. Such examples include *Return of the Dove to the Ark* by Millais which the artist painted to suit a High Church friend and which gives a completely new interpretation to the biblical story of the Deluge, with emphasis on the daughters of Noah greeting the bird. In two works by Rossetti, *The Annunciation* and *The Girlhood of Mary*, the white dove appears as holy messenger in the former and as a haloed pigeon sitting on a garden fence in the other. He also includes the white lily representing the purity and innocence of the Virgin Mary, together with the unusual feature of a red hanging cloth on which, in early legend, Mary was said to have been working in the Temple. The artist's intention in both works was to portray feminine excellence. In *The Annunciation* he paints Mary as a vision of spotless maidenhood and spiritual perfection, although shrinking from the reality of the angel's message (see page 148). In *The Girlhood of Mary* she is shown being instructed by St Ann. The books in the foreground are inscribed with the names of the cardinal virtues, faith, hope, charity and fortitude, presumably regarded as desirable womanly virtues. Rossetti was neither a believing nor a professing Christian, but in dealing with religious subjects he was sympathetic and indeed reverent in tone.

The third member, William Holman Hunt, was inspired by reading Ruskin's *Modern Painters* and was the last artist to join the Brotherhood. He had a strong religious commitment and followed Ruskin's concept of the author as explorer, but always with a moral obligation in mind to serve God. He made several journeys to the Near East, especially to the Holy Land and also to Egypt. His use of symbolism in promoting the Christian cause was not always appreciated, but his most famous painting, *Light of the World*, became the most popular Protestant picture of the 19th century.

The Return of the Dove
to the Ark *by John
Everett Millais, showing
the daughters of Noah
receiving back the dove.
(Ashmolean Museum,
Oxford)*

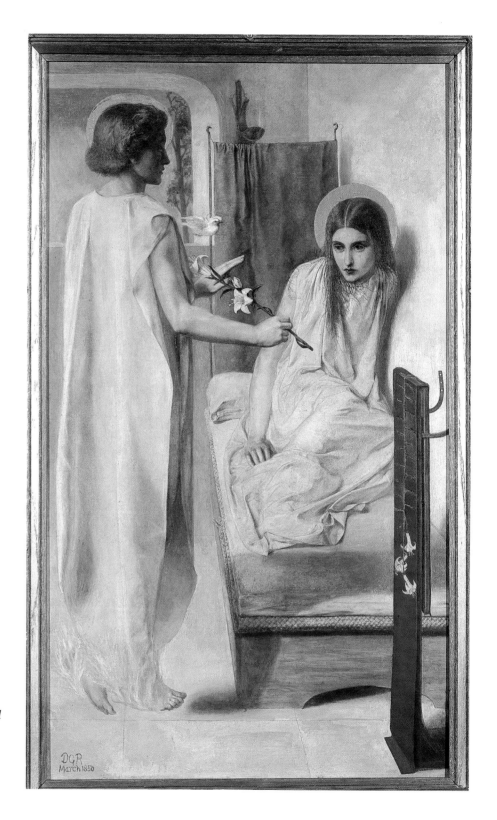

The Annunciation *by Dante Gabriel Rossetti showing an interpretation of the Virgin's reaction to the angel's daunting message.*
(© Tate, London 2002)

The Afterglow in Egypt was begun in Giza and completed in 1863 and was the first of his life-sized female figures. It may be that the subject was an allegorical interpretation of natural abundance in a decayed civilisation, but Holman Hunt denied that there was "any kind or degree of mysticism in the painting". The inclusion of several breeds of fancy pigeon in this and another painting, *The Festival of St Swithin*, suggests that he might have been familiar with the birds in a domestic context (see next page).

Although not a founder member of the Pre-Raphaelite movement, William Morris was in sympathy with its aims, particularly in his admiration for the values of the medieval world. His active and enquiring mind led him to take an interest in a wide variety of arts and

The Afterglow in Egypt *by William Holman Hunt, depicting several fancy pigeons. (Southampton City Art Gallery, Hampshire, UK/Bridgeman Art Library)*

(right) The Festival of St Swithin by William Holman Hunt. A dove-cote is shown inhabited by several varieties of pigeon. (Ashmolean Museum, Oxford)

Tile panel depicting a pair of facing doves amongst flowers and foliage, by William de Morgan. (V&A Picture Library)

crafts, some long neglected, as well as in the social and economic conditions of the day. Over the years, however, his extraordinary skill as a designer was his outstanding contribution to art and this is a legacy that has endured. In 1861, he founded the firm Morris & Co., which became one of the finest stained glass makers of the 19th century, chiefly in its choice of deep colours not found in medieval glass. The firm also made furniture, wallpaper and tapestry. His famous designs for the flat patterns of the firm's wallpapers, later used in carpets, drew their inspiration from nature. Being further involved in book design, his work entitled *A Book of Verse*, published in 1870, was sent as a birthday present to his close friend and confidante Georgiana Burne-Jones. The texts are written by Morris himself and reveal his skills as poet and calligrapher; the pictures are by Charles F. Murray. The poem *Praise of Venus* includes three delicate miniatures of the goddess set in the countryside and in a seascape; her white doves fly about her in two of them.

The influence of Morris & Co. in Europe and North America was the forerunner of a host of guilds and societies that made up the Arts and Crafts movement. William de Morgan (1839-1917) was one of the most original artist-craftsmen associated with this trend. He was particularly interested in the artistic and technical aspects of ceramic decoration. His main productions were tiles with floral and foliate patterns in the style of William Morris, as can be seen in an example incorporating a pair of doves.

(left) Dove and rose design, incorporating the facing dove motif, for a woven wool and silk fabric by William Morris for Morris & Company in 1879.
(photography copyright William Morris Gallery, London)

(below) Altar panel with doves, designed by Mary Watts for the Mortuary Chapel of the Royal Cambridge Military Hospital in Aldershot.
(photograph by Russell Towns)

Mary Seton Watts, who in 1898 designed the Watts Chapel in Compton, Surrey, which contains a wealth of symbolic images, was also a follower of the Arts and Crafts movement. Her altar panel for the Mortuary Chapel of the Royal Cambridge Military Hospital, Aldershot, depicts doves and foliage around the central cross with alpha and omega on either side.

The painter and decorative artist Edward Burne-Jones (1833-1898) was a leading figure in the second phase of the Pre-Raphaelite Movement. He met William Morris at Cambridge and was also influenced by Ruskin, who introduced him to Italian painting. In his series of four paintings for the story of Pygmalion and Galatea known as *The Godhead Fires* he contrasted physical desire with aesthetic ideals. The Greek legend tells the story of the King of Cyprus who fell in love with his statue of the ideal woman which the goddess Venus (Aphrodite) eventually brought to life so that he could marry it. In one scene, numerous doves, many carrying roses, fly around the figure of Venus while Galatea on

Venus and Galatea, *the painting known as the Godhead Fires, part of the story of Pygmalion and Galatea by Edward Burne-Jones. (Birmingham Museums & Art Gallery)*

her plinth comes to life. Stained glass was his particular forte and he produced an endless flow of cartoons for the firm of W. Morris, which he helped to found. There are several fine examples of his work in the chapel of Jesus College, Cambridge, one depicting the dove with an olive branch returning to Noah while another shows a dove perched on the shoulder of Solomon (see pages 70 & 74). His pen-and-ink version of *The Baptism of Christ* for a stained-glass window at St

Return of the Dove to the Ark *by
Edward Burne-Jones, an unusually
macabre interpretation.*
(V&A Picture Library)

Edmund Hall, Oxford follows the traditional theme, but his macabre illustration
for *The Return of the Dove to the Ark* dwells on more grotesque details of man and
creatures drowning in the Deluge. He also produced designs for furniture, tapestry,
seals, needlework and jewellery. The latter included a most elegant brooch in
the form of a dove, which Lady Burne-Jones in her biography described as "the
only piece of jewellery Burne-Jones completely designed and saw executed".

Walter Crane (1845-1915) was a painter, book illustrator and designer who also worked on wood engravings with Morris at the Kelmscott Press. During a protracted Italian honeymoon from 1871-1873, he evolved a personal style of gouache landscape painting which he simplified to convey the sun-baked character of the Italian countryside. Crane's larger-scale pictures increasingly reflected his belief that art might be used as a metaphor for the human condition. *The Renaissance of Venus*, the largest oil-painting that he had undertaken at that time, both shows his study of Botticelli and underlines his hopes that a new appreciation of beauty in art and decoration was evolving in England.

The Renaissance of Venus *by Walter Crane. The artist has clearly been influenced by the work of Sandro Botticelli. The painting was first shown at the Grosvenor Gallery in 1877 and bought by the painter G. F. Watts.* (© *Tate, London 2002*)

Several followers of the Movement depicted the dove in less aesthetic and more down-to-earth guises, but nevertheless in beguiling and attractive ways. Arthur Hughes (1832-1915) was converted to Pre-Raphaelism in 1850 while a student, and was a friend of Millais to whom he was indebted, together with Hunt and Rossetti, as exemplars. As well as medieval subjects he was inspired to portray the tender feelings of childhood, often combined with details of flowers, animals and birds. In addition, he produced a number of more formal group portraits, which lacked the intimate mood of the early paintings, for example *Portrait of Mrs Leathart with three Children*. In this work the detail of the fancy breeds of pigeon reveals a delightful familiarity with the birds.

Portrait of Mrs Leathart with three Children by Arthur Hughes. This charming domestic scene reveals a familiarity with different breeds of pigeons. (Laing Art Gallery, Tyne and Wear Museums, Newcastle-upon-Tyne)

The Pigeon *by Joseph Crawhall.*
(Glasgow Museums: The Burrell
Collection)

Joseph Crawhall (1861-1913) specialised in painting bird, animal and humorous subjects. Although working in oils initially, he later abandoned the technique and began to use gouache, which he painted on brown Holland cloth after 1888. His chief patron was William Burrell who owned more of his work than that of any other artist. The painting of *The Pigeon*, with its subtle detail and shading and wonderfully shining eye, is now in the Sir William Burrell Collection in Glasgow.

As well as portraying the dove in day-to-day life, a popular theme in Victorian imagery was to use the bird allegorically in a feminine role with its association of tenderness and vulnerability. Rebecca Solomon (1832-1886) echoes this trend in *The Wounded Dove*, painted in 1866. She was the sister of the Pre-Raphaelite painter Simeon and the genre painter Abraham, and is best known for her portraits and history paintings. She worked both in the studio of Millais and for Burne-Jones, the latter in the capacity of a model.

In 2002, the National Trust acquired the astonishingly intact Victorian house and chapel at Tyntesfield, Somerset, which was built for William Gibbs who had made a fortune from importing bird guano. This picturesque Gothic-style country house has a fine ensemble of architecture, art and gardens and contains a charming sculpture of Gibbs's youngest daughter with a dove.

The British sculptor, Sir Jacob Epstein, was born in North America in 1880 and spent his childhood in New York, but after brief spells in Paris he settled in Britain. In developing a fresh approach he adopted the procedure of direct carving, which for him meant cultivating a close relationship with his material. This idea represented his feeling of 'truth to materials', which involved preserving the colour and texture or markings as aesthetic elements in themselves. In 1912, Epstein settled in the remote village of Pett Level on the Sussex coast to concentrate on his sculpting. During this prolific period he combined the influence of Modigliani and Brancusi, together with African carvings which he had seen in the British Museum, to express the theme of sexuality. He was also influenced by Brancusi in taking the unprecedented step of basing major works of sculpture on animal rather than human imagery. Doves, as a traditional symbol of love, peace and fertility, were a perfect subject for interpretation in a

(above left) The Wounded Dove
by Rebecca Solomon.
(The University of Wales,
Aberystwyth)

(above right) One of the treasures of
the National Trust at Tyntesfield,
Somerset, is the charming marble
sculpture of the original owner's
daughter holding a dove.
(Country Life)

157

style free from sentimentality, which focused on the unambiguous act of procreation. Epstein kept doves at his cottage and made sketches of them, which were then worked up into the more formal design of the mating doves. He carved three pairs in white Parian marble.

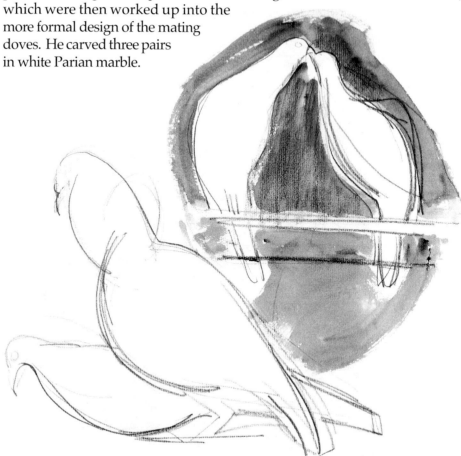

Sketch of Doves by Jacob Epstein.
(The Garman Ryan Collection,
The New Art Gallery, Walsall)

The sculptor Barbara Hepworth, born at the turn of the century, was also influenced by the concept of 'truth to materials' but in addition she was impressed by the early Cycladic carvers. Her sculptured *Doves* in marble appeared in an exhibition in 1928, a few years after she had left the Royal College of Art. It is possible that the work was inspired by her various stays in Italy during that period.

Sculpture of mating doves in white Parian marble by Jacob Epstein. (Hirschhorn Museum and Sculpture Garden, Smithsonian Institute, Washington, DC, gift of Joseph H. Hirschhorn, 1966, photograph by Lee Stalsworth)

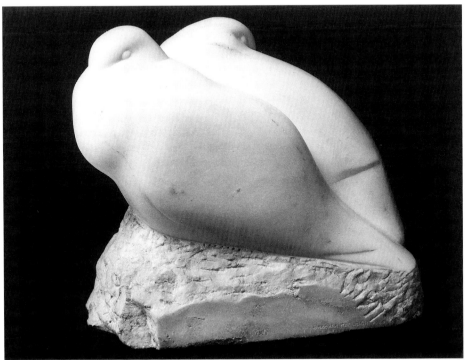

Doves by Barbara Hepworth, an early sculpture in Parian marble, 1927. (© Bowness, Hepworth Estate and Manchester Art Gallery)

159

The English painter and graphic artist, Frank Brangwyn, was born in Bruges, where his father was an ecclesiastical architect and textile designer. He moved to England in 1875 and later travelled abroad to Europe, the Near East and Africa, acquiring an international reputation. He had a broad

Baptism of Christ *in a stained-glass window by Frank Brangwyn, executed by Tiffany & Co. of New York.*
(The Baltimore Museum of Art, gift of Herman & Rosa L. Cohen, and Ben & Zelda G. Cohen, BMA 1979.5)

knowledge of Dutch and Flemish art and his style was influenced by the Pre-Raphaelites as well as Delacroix, Titian, Veronese and European symbolists. He received many mural commissions, both in Britain and abroad, including 16 panels for the chapel of Christ's Hospital School at Horsham, representing scenes depicting the spread of the gospel. In these and other works he shows his keen observation of nature in which he expressed his philosophy of art as the means to unite man, God and creation. His stained-glass window of the *Baptism of Christ* showing the dove encircled by a colourful halo and rays, was executed by Tiffany & Co of New York.

The style known as Art Deco which flourished roughly from 1910-1939, though mainly after the First World War, was characterised by geometric motifs, curvilinear forms and sharply defined outlines. Although found worldwide, it had no agreed doctrine but epitomised an era and an atmosphere as much as an artistic movement. It has been conjectured that it reflected a reaction to the horrors of war on the one hand and an attempt to close the gap between art and industry on the other. A cover of *Vogue* and the design of a fan reflect the taste of the time, while *Les Perruches*, a

painting by Jean Dupas, from 1925, depicts the parakeets of the title together with a central female figure in black and three female nudes, one of which holds a dove. Three white doves in flight are also included (see next page).

(left) A cover of Vogue *magazine from 1926, in Art Deco style. (V&A Picture Library)*

(below) A lady's fan in the form of a dove, gouache on textured paper, 1920. (V&A Picture Library)

Les Perruches *by Jean Dupas (1882-1964), designed for the 1925 Exposition des Arts Decoratifs et Industriels, Paris, the original Art Deco exhibition. There are parakeets in the centre, three doves on the left and one held by the nude female on the right.*
(© Christie's Images Ltd., 2003)

Piccione Primavera *by Ercole Barovier, glass, 1930.*
(by courtesy of Angelo Barovier, Barovier e Toso, Venice)

In the 1920s and 1930s, Venetian glass produced on the island of Murano was regularly featured at the Venice Biennales. One of the leading innovators in modernising the designs used and moving away from the traditional filigree work produced on Murano was the Barovier family workshop. Their designers produced many images of birds and animals in glass and in 1930, Ercole Barovier exhibited a particularly witty version of a pigeon at the Biennale.

The working career of Eric Gill extended from 1908-1940 during which time he became interested in typography and also produced many wood engravings. Included among these were many human figures with curvilinear forms which at the time were labelled indecent or erotic. However, he was a deeply religious man and to him art was "man's act of collaboration with God in creating". It is not surprising, therefore, that he portrayed the dove of the Holy Spirit in several engravings, including one in a commemorative stamp for the League of Nations.

162

The Spanish artist, Antoni Gaudi, born in 1852, studied in Barcelona and worked initially as a draughtsman. Amongst his later work was the Templo Expiatorio de la Sagra Familia in Barcelona, a work of architectural surrealism, which is considered to be among the most impressive buildings of the 20th century. The main façade is dominated by four towers named after the apostles, while the three shaggy portals represent Faith, Hope and Charity. Above the central portal is the Tree of Life covered with white doves, an echo of the symbolism of Christian and pre-Christian days.

Pablo Picasso, the Spanish painter, sculptor, draughtsman, print-maker and decorative artist, dominated 20th-century European art and became one of the most significant artists of the century. He was born in Malaga in 1881 and moved north with his family to Catalonia when he was 13. He received his first lessons in painting from his father, José Ruiz Blasco, a painter specialising in pictures of pigeons and doves and a teacher at the local school of fine arts. He recognised and encouraged his son's aptitude at an early age. The preserved drawings that Picasso produced as a child of nine display a precocious grasp of naturalistic conventions. Some of them also reflect his father's repertory as can be seen in the sketches of pigeons which accompany, almost as an afterthought, Pablo's drawings of a bull-fight. There is a story that his elderly father, whose eyesight was failing, asked his son to help him finish the intricate bits of his painting of a pigeon. He chopped off the claws and nailed them to a board. The result was painted with such skill that the father handed over his palette, brushes and paint and declared that he would never paint again.

(left) The tree of life with doves at the Templo Expiatorio de la Sagra Familia, Barcelona, by Antoni Gaudi. (photograph by Tim Graham)

Two wood-engravings by Eric Gill: (upper) the dove as the Holy Spirit; (lower) a design for a stamp to commemorate the League of Nations. (V&A Picture Library)

La Corrida y Seis Estudios de Palomas, *an early sketch by Pablo Picasso.*
(© Succession Picasso/DACS 2003. Museu Picasso, Barcelona, © Photo Arxio Fotogràfic de Museus, Ajuntament de Barcelona)

Picasso made France his permanent home and lived in Paris during the Nazi Occupation. He led a turbulent, emotional life and in 1943 began a relationship with François Gilot, who in her *Life with Picasso* describes the kitchen of their Paris apartment, in which he kept pigeons, canaries and turtle doves that were free to fly about. There seems little doubt that he retained his affection for the pigeon throughout his life as numerous light-hearted and

(above) Lithograph of La Paloma
by Pablo Picasso, 1949.
(© Succession Picasso/DACS 2003.
Museu Picasso, Barcelona,
© Photo Arxio Fotogràfic de Museus,
Ajuntament de Barcelona)

(below) Dove and Rainbow *by*
Pablo Picasso.
(The University of Wales,
Aberystwyth)

affectionate drawings, lithographs and paintings reveal. In 1944, soon after the Liberation, he joined the Communist Party, to which he made substantial donations. He also made a lithograph of his famous pigeon for the Communist-sponsored Peace Congress, which became a world icon representing 'Peace and Goodwill'. In reality it was probably one of four Milanese pigeons given to him by Matisse.

Child with Dove *by Pablo Picasso.*
(© The National Gallery, London)

165

A major exhibition in 1998 at the Royal Academy of Arts drew fresh
attention to Picasso's ceramic works. In it he is seen to have transformed
everyday objects in an imaginative, inventive and often witty fusion of
sculpture and painting, also influenced by ancient traditions and mythology. Several examples of the dove in white earthenware, sometimes
with added details in slip, were exhibited. There were also simple pots in
the form of a dove in which the neck of the vessel was bent back to form
the head and then pulled forward to make the bird's beak. Picasso is

reported to have said: "You see, to make a dove, you must wring its neck."
Late in his long life, Picasso lived in the south of France. At his villa, he
made a colourful series of paintings of his pigeons, entitled *Los Pichons*.
The birds are seen perched mainly on his balcony overlooking the sea,
and have built-in nestholes alongside, some of which are seen occupied
by nesting birds.

The intermittent rivalry between the French painter, draughtsman, sculptor and printmaker Henri Matisse and Picasso was a lasting feature of their careers. In response to criticism of his work and to Picasso's challenge for the leadership of the avant-garde, Matisse published his own artist's credo. In spite of this friction, however, both artists shared a love of pigeons and François Gilot, writing about a visit with Picasso to Matisse, described the four Milanese pigeons that were kept with other exotic birds in his aviary: "Their feet were not bare like other pigeons, they had feathers right down to their claws, it was just as though the feet had white gaiters on." On another occasion, Matisse said that he would give the birds to Picasso because they "look like some you have already painted". A photograph of Matisse in old age shows him with a bird of this type on his shoulder.

René Magritte was the most paradoxical of the surrealists. By turning normality on its head, he reversed the usual expectations and so revealed the ordinary in the extraordinary. At the same time, he emphasised the tension between reality and illusion. Magritte, who was a painter, print-maker, sculptor, photographer and filmmaker, was born in Belgium and studied at the Academie des Beaux-Arts, Brussels. In spite of his ideas of releasing man from conventional bourgeois life, he himself led a conformist existence with a devoted wife, who is shown in an early photograph with pigeons on her shoulders. Magritte's first surrealist works were shown in the 1920s and it was at this time that he created standardised human types, favouring especially the bowler-hatted man, who made the first of many appearances in 1927. He later introduced a mythological interpretation to his work as can been seen in *La Magie Noire* and

La Domaine Enchantée II *by René Magritte, one of a series of paintings from Knokke, 1953. Female figure with white dove and an entwined serpent motif behind.* (© *Photothèque R. Magritte/ ADAGP, Paris, 2003*)

the wall-painting at Knokke, in both of which the image of the ancient goddess is seen with her dove and in the latter also her symbolical serpents entwined as a pair of castles. Many different interpretations of his work have been made, but Magritte himself neatly summarised his feelings on the subject in this way:

> It is rather pointless to put one's hopes in a dogmatic point
> of view, since it is the power of enchantment which matters.

La Magie Noire *by René Magritte. 1934. The female nude beside the sea with a white dove on her shoulder recalls early mythological links.* (© *ADAGP, Paris and DACS, London 2003. Private Collection/ Bridgeman Art Library)*

(right) The Therapeutist *by René Magritte, 1937.*
The caged doves appear in an enigmatic role.
(© ADAGP, Paris and DACS, London 2003.
Private Collection/Bridgeman Art Library)

(below) L'homme au chapeau Melon *by René Magritte, 1964.*
The bowler-hatted man with white dove.
(© Photothèque R. Magritte/ADAGP, Paris, 2003)

James Lynch is a contemporary Somerset-based painter with a penchant for birds and animals. In his own words: "I've always painted landscapes, then the animals got in, and they got bigger and bigger..." He "always works from the sky downward" and recalls weekends as a child of keen amateur pilots "looking up at the sky, waiting for my parents to drop out of it". The two paintings on pages 172 & 173 accurately reflect these influences.

The dove as a symbol has endured for centuries and although the emphasis has changed it seems likely to continue to do so in the future. In this age of consumerism it features widely on greetings cards of all kinds, with or without the traditional message of peace and reconciliation, and is even incorporated into advertisements. But it still holds a place in con-

(left) The Peace Fountain by Charles Gagnon in Rochester, New York.

(below) A recent glass engraving of the dove as the Holy Spirit by John Hutton at the Chapel of Thanksgiving in Dallas, Texas. (by kind permission of Marigold Hutton)

temporary civic sculpture, as can be seen in the Peace Fountain in Rochester, New York, created by Charles Gagnon in 1989. It is made of circular tiers of bronze doves representing the 50 states and seven continents.

The dove's religious significance has also not been forgotten as can be seen in recent glass engravings by John Hutton at the rebuilt Coventry Cathedral where St Columba is depicted carrying a dove and St David is shown with a dove about to alight on his shoulder, while more recently at the Chapel of Thanksgiving in Dallas, Texas, the dove as Holy Spirit has an accompanying note:

> The Dove is a symbol throughout history depicting beauty, peace, hope and thanksgiving.

171

Doves flying above a brick outhouse with upper-storey dovecote at Tytherington, Wiltshire, by James Lynch, 1995.
(by courtesy of James Lynch)

*Doves in flight
above Rainscombe
House, Wiltshire,
by James Lynch,
1998.
(by courtesy of
James Lynch)*

173

BIBLIOGRAPHY

Abul Fazl 'Allami, *The Ain Akbari*, vols I & VI (H. Blochman, trans.), Calcutta (1873)

Aesop's Fables, with Proverbs and Applications, Bliss & Sands, London (1897)

Alciatus, Andreas, *Emblematum Fontes Quator* (H. Green, ed. from original edition of 1531), Holbein Society, London (1870)

Anderson, M.D., *History and Imagery in British Churches*, John Murray, London (1971)

Anglicus, Bartholomaeus, *Medieval Lore: an Epitome of the Science ... and Myth of the Middle Ages ... Gleanings from the Encyclopedia of Bartholomew Anglicus on the Properties of Things* (Robert Steele, ed., with a preface by William Morris), Elliot Stock, London (1893)

Ashton, John, *The Voiage and Travayle of Sir John Maundeville*, Knight, Pickering & Chatto, London (1887)

Attwater, Donald, *The Penguin Dictionary of Saints*, Penguin, Harmondsworth (1965)

Backhouse, Robert (ed.), *Christian Martyrs*, Hodder & Stoughton, London (1996)

Baring, Anne & Cashford, Jules, *The Myth of the Goddess*, Penguin Books, London (1991)

Barchusan (also Barckhausen), J.G., *Elementa Chemiae*, Lugduni Batavorum (1718)

Bartlett, Robert (Ed.), *Medieval Panorama*, Thames & Hudson, London (2001)

Bartoli, Pietro Santi, *Le Antiche Lucerne Sepolcrali Figurati ...*, part 3, G.F. Buagni, Roma (1691)

Batiffol, Pierre, *Saint Gregory the Great*, Burns, Oates, London (1929)

Biedermann, Hans, *The Wordsworth Dictionary of Symbolism*, Wordsworth, Ware (1996)

Boas, George (trans.), *The Hieroglyphics of Horapollo*, Pantheon Books, New York (1950)

Bodio, Stephen, *Aloft: a meditation on Pigeons and Pigeon Flying*, Pruett Publishing Co., Boulder, Colorado (1993)

Boccaccio, Giovanni, *Bocace de la Généalogie des dieux*, I. Petit, Paris (1531)

Boghossian, Sarkis, *Armenian Iconography*, Boghossian, Paris (1987)

Bond, Francis, *Dedications and Patron Saints of English Churches*, Oxford University Press, London (1914)

The Book of Saints, A. & C. Black, London (1989)

Bosio, Antonio, *Roma Sotteranea*, vols. 3 & 4, G. Facciotti, Roma (1632)

Bovini, Giuseppe & Pierpaoli, Mario (Manuela Farneli, trans.) *Ravenna: Treasures of Light*, Longo, Ravenna (2000)

Boyd, Graeme R., 'Picasso's Pigeons', *Feathered World*, vol.10 (1993)

Boyd, Henry (trans.), *The Triumphs of Francesco Petrarch*, John Murray, London (1906)

Briggs, Geoffrey, *National Heraldry of the World*, Dent, London (1973)

Bryant, Jacob, *A New System or an Analysis of Ancient Mythology*, vol. 3, J. Walker, London (1807)

Budge, E.A. Wallis. *One Hundred and Ten Miracles of Our Lady Mary*, Medici Society, London (1923)

Cabrol, Fernand, *Dictionnaire d'Archéologie Chrétienne et de Liturgie*, vol. 3, Paris (1914)

Camerario, Ioachimo, *Symbolorum et Emblematum*, Ammonii, Frankfurt (1654)

Carter Harry (trans.), *The Histories of Herodotus*, Oxford University Press, Oxford (1962)

Caws, Mary Ann, *Dora Maar: with and without Picasso*, Thames & Hudson, London (2000)

Chamberlain F., *The Homing Pigeon*, Homing Pigeon Publishing Co., Manchester (1907)

Chambers, J.D. (trans.), *Hermes Trismegistus*, T. & T. Clark, Edinburgh (1882)

Chapman, Frank M., 'Chinese Pigeon Whistles', *National Geographic Magazine*, (June 1931)

Child, Heather and Colles, Dorothy, *Christian Symbols Ancient and Modern*, George Bell, London (1971)

Cook, A.O., *Zeus, God of the Bright Sky*, Cambridge University Press, Cambridge (1914)

Cooper, J.C., *An Illustrated Encyclopedia of Traditional Symbols*, Thames & Hudson, London (1978)

Cory, Alexander Turner (ed.), *The Hieroglyphics of Horapollo Nilous* (Greek version with English translation), William Pickering, London (1839)

Crescentio, Pietro, *De Agricultura*, book 9, Sansovino, Venice (1561)

Cresswell, Richard, *Aristotle's History of Animals*, book IX, Bohn's Classical History, London (1862)

Creuzer, Georg F., *Symbolik und Mythologie der alter Volken*, vol. 4, Paris (1810)

Crosnier, Augustin J., *Iconographie Chrétienne*, Paris & Caen (1848)

Dalbanne, Claude (ed.), *La nouvelle Légende Dorée*, Lyons edition of 1483, Lyons (1924)

Davis, J.I. (ed.), *Libellus de Natura Animalium*, Dawsons, London (1958)

Daremberg, Charles V. & Saglio, Edmond, *Dictionnaire des Antiquités Grecques et Romaines*, 5 volumes, Hachette, Paris (1873-1919)

Delehaye, Hippolyte, *Legends of the Saints* (Donald Attwater, trans.), Geoffrey Chapman, London (1962)

Didron, Adolphe M., *Christian Iconography*, vols. I. & II, Henry G. Bohn, London (1851)

Evans, Arthur, *The Palace of Minos*, vols. 1 & 2, Macmillan, London (1921)

Evans, Helen C. & Wixom, William D., *The Glory of Byzantium: Art and Culture of the Middle Byzantine Era (AD 843-1261)*, The Metropolitan Museum of Art, New York (1997)

Farmer, David Hugh, *The Oxford Dictionary of Saints*, Oxford University Press, Oxford (1987)

Fernando, Diana, *Alchemy: An Illustrated A to Z*, Blandford, London (1998)

Fludd, Robert, *Utriusque: Cosmi Majoris ...* , Oppenheim, Frankfurt (1617-26)

Fontana, David, *The Secret Language of Symbols*, Duncain Baird Publishers, London (1993)

Frazer, James G. (commentary by), *Pausanias' Description of Greece*, 6 vols., Macmillan, London (1913)

Freeman, Rosemary, *English Emblem Books*, Chatto & Windus, London (1948)

Gablik, Suzi, *Magritte*, Thames and Hudson, London (1977)

Garrucci, Raffaele, *Storia dell'Arte Cristiana* (vols. 2, 3, 4, 5 & 6) Prato (1872-99)

Gerhard, Eduard, *Etruskische Spiegel*, Georg Reimer, Berlin (1840-67)

Gesell, Geraldine, *Town, Palace and House Cult in Minoan Crete*, Aströms, Göteborg (1985)

Goldsmith, Elisabeth, *Ancient Pagan Symbols*, Archibald Constable & Co., London (1907)

Goodenough, E.R., *Jewish Symbols in the Greco-Roman Period* (vols. I, VII & VIII), Pantheon Books, New York (1953)

Haag-Wackernagel, Daniel, *Die Taube*, Schwabe, Basel (1998)

Hall, James, *A History of Ideas and Images in Italian Art*, John Murray, London (1983)

Hall, James, *Dictionary of Subjects and Symbols in Art*, John Murray, London (1984)

Hall, James, *Illustrated Dictionary of Symbols in Eastern and Western Art*, John Murray, London (1994)

Hansell, Jean, *The Pigeon in History*, Millstream Books, Bath (1998)

Hardy, Eric, *A-Z Pigeon Guide*, Burke, London (1951)

Herrad de Landsberg, *Hortus Deliciarum*, Strasbourg, Paris (1952)

Holder, Heidi, *Aesop's Fables*, Macmillan, London (1981)

Hoose, H.P., *Peking Pigeons and Pigeon Flutes*, Peking (1938)

Hrabanus, Magnentius, *Miniature Sacre e Profano dell Anno 1023 illustranti l'enciclopedia medioevale di Rabano Mauro*, Montecassino (1896)

Husenbeth, Frederick C., *Emblems of Saints*, Longman, London (1860)

Jameson, Anna B., *Legends of the Monastic Orders*, Hutchinson, London (1852)

Jameson, Anna B., *Sacred and Legendary Art*, Longman, London (1883)

Jashemski, Wilhelmina F., *The Gardens of Pompeii, Herculaneum & Villas Destroyed by Vesuvius*, Caratzas, New Rochelle (1979 & 1993)

Jenner, Katherine L. *Christian Symbolism*, Methuen, London (1910)

Jung, Carl G., *Collected works of C.G. Jung*, vol. 12, Routledge & Kegan Paul, London & New York (1954)

Kaftal, George, *Iconography of the Saints in Tuscan Painting*, Sansoni, Florence (1952)

Katzenellenbogen, Adolf, *Allegories of the Virtues and Vices in Medieval Art*, University of Toronto Press, Toronto (1989)

Klingender, Francis, *Animals in Art and Thought to the end of the Middle Ages*, Routledge & Kegan Paul, London (1971)

Knight, Richard Payne, *An Inquiry into the Symbolical Language of Ancient Art and Mythology*, privately printed, London (1818)

La Croix, Paul, *The Arts in the Middle Ages and the Renaissance*, Random House, London (1996)

La Fontaine, The Fables of (R. Thomson, trans. from French), Nimmo & Bain, London (1884)

Lassus, Jean B.A., *Album de Villard de Honnecourt*, Paris (1858)

Lauts, Jan, *Carpaccio: Paintings and Drawings*, Phaidon, London (1962)

Lehner, Ernst, *Symbols, Signs and Signets*, The World Publishing Co., New York (1950)

Leonard, John, *Churches of Herefordshire and their Treasures*, Logaston Press, Almeley (2000)

Leonte, Ovidiu, *Porumbei Galateni*, Bucharest (1992)

MacLagan, Eric, *The Bayeux Tapestry*, Penguin, Harmondsworth (1943)

Mâle, Emile, *L'Art religieux du XIIIe siècle en France*, Paris (1919)

Marle, Raimond van, *Iconographie de l'Art Profane au Moyen Age ...* , Martinus Nijhoff, The Hague (1932)

Marsh, Jan, *Pre-Raphaelite Women*, Weidenfeld & Nicholson, London (1987)

Mandeville, Sir John, *The Voyages and Travels of Sir John Mandevile Knight*, R. Scott, T. Basset, London (1684)

Maoloni, Ambrosia, *La Palombella*, Azienda di Promozione Turistica dell' Orvietano, Orvieto (1996)

Matino, Renzo, *Ravenna, City of Art*, Editions Salbaroli, Ravenna (1998)

Mesnil du Buisson, Robert du, *Nouvelles études sur les dieux et les mythes de Canaan*, E.J Brill, Leiden (1974)

Montfaucon, Bernard de, *L'Antiquité expliquée et représentée en figures*, vol.1, book 5, Delaulne, Paris (1719)

Murray, Peter and Linda, *The Oxford Companion to Christian Art and Architecture*, Oxford University Press, Oxford (1996)

Musavi, Sayid Muhammad Valih, *Kabutarnama (The History of Pigeons)*, Ms Islamic 4811, Oriental and India Office Collections, British Library, London (1770)

Neumann, Erich, *The Great Mother: An Analysis of the Archetype*, Routledge & Kegan Paul, London (1955)

Ordish, George and Binder, Pearl, *Pigeons and People*, Dennis Dobson, London (1967)

Osman, A.H., *Pigeons in the Great War*, Racing Pigeon Publishing Co., London (1918)

Osman, W.H., *Pigeons in World War II*, Racing Pigeon Publishing Co., London (1950)

Panofsky, Erwin, *Studies in Iconology*, Oxford University Press, New York (1939)

Panofsky, Erwin, *Renaissance and Renascences in Western Art*, Harper & Row, London & New York (1972)

Parmelee, Alice, *All the Birds of the Bible*, Lutterworth, London (1959)

Pekanovic, Josip, 'The Coming of the Domestic Pigeon', *Feathered World*, vol. 14, no. 6 (1997)

Pekanovic, Josip, 'Vukovar's Hen Pigeon', *Feathered World*, vol. 15, no. 8 (1998)

Ripa, Cesare, *Iconologia del Cesare Ripa*, Padua (1630)

Ripa, Cesare, *Iconologia or Moral Emblems*, London (1709)

Rochelle, Mercedes, *Post-Biblical Saints Art Index*, McFarland, London & Jefferson, North Carolina (c.1994)

Rose, Martial & Hedgecoe, Julia, *Stories in Stone*, Thames & Hudson, London (1997)

Rupin, Ernest, *L'Oeuvre de Limoges*, Alphonse Picard, Paris (1890)

Sabbagh, Mikha'il, *La Colombe Messagère plus rapide que l'éclair plus prompte que la nue* (A.I. Silvestre de Sacy, trans.), Imprimerie Impériale, Paris (1805)

Sansoni, G.C. (ed.), *World Encyclopedia of Art*, vols. I, II, III, IV, V, VII, IX & XI, McGraw Hill, New York (1958-1968)

Saurma-Jeltsch, Lieselotte E., *Die Miniaturen im 'Liber Scivias' der Hildegard von Bingen*, Reichert, Wiesbaden (1998)

Schiller, Gertrud, *Iconography of Christian Art* (Janet Seligman trans.), vols. I & II, Lund Humphries, London (1972)

Schneir, Jacques, 'The Symbolic Bird in Medieval and Renaissance Art', *The American Imago*, vol. 9, no. 1 April (1952)

Scott, Thomas D. (ed.), *The Fables of Pilpay*, Lumley, London (1852)

Scruton, Roger, *England: an Elegy*, Chatto & Windus, London (2000)

Sewter, A. Charles, *The Stained Glass of William Morris and his Circle*, Yale University Press, New Haven & London (1974-5)

Seznec, Jean, *The Survival of the Pagan Gods*, Warburg Institute, London (1940)

Simms, Eric, *The Public Life of the Street Pigeon*, Hutchinson, London (1979)

Smith, D.J., *Roman Mosaics at Hull*, City of Hull Museums & Art Galleries (1987)

Smith, William & Cheetham, Samuel, *Dictionary of Christian Antiquities*, John Murray, London (1890)

Smith, William, *Dictionary of Greek and Roman Antiquities*, John Murray, London (1875)

Speake, Jennifer, *The Dent Dictionary of Symbols in Christian Art*, Dent, London (1994)

Spivey, Nigel, *Etruscan Art*, Thames & Hudson, London (1997)

Taylor, Thomas, *The Life of St Samson of Dol*, SPCK, London (1925)

Tervarent, Guy de, *Attributs et symboles dans l'art profane, 1450-1600*, Droz, Geneva (1958)

Tischbein, Johann H.W., *Collection of Engravings from ancient Vases ...* , vols. II & III, Naples (1791-955)

Townsend, G.F., *The Fables of Aesop*, Warne, London (1866)

Trismosin, Salomon, *Splendor Solis*, Kegan Paul, London (1920)

Turner, Jane (ed.), *The Dictionary of Art*, 34 vols., Macmillan, London (1996)

Twining, Louisa, *Symbols and Emblems of Early and Mediaeval Christian Art*, John Murray, London (1885)

Utley, Gertje R., *Picasso: the Communist Years*, Yale University Press, New Haven & London (2000)

Vinycomb, John, *Fictitious and Symbolic Creatures in Art*, Chapman & Hall, London (1906)

Von Franz, Marie Louise (commentary by), *Aurora Consurgens*, Routledge & Kegan Paul, London (1966)

Voragine, Jacobus de, *Leaves from the Golden Legend*, Archibald Constable, London (1898)

Wade-Evans, Arthur W. (ed.), *Life of Saint David*, SPCK, London (1923)

Walters, H.B., *Catalogue of the Greek and Etruscan Vases in the British Museum*, vol. IV, Department of Greek and Roman Antiquities, British Museum London (1893)

Weitzman, Kurt. and Kessler Herbert L. (eds.), *The Cotton Genesis*, vol. 1, Princeton University Press, Princeton (1986)

Whitbread, Leslie G. (trans.), *Fulgentius the Mythographer*, Ohio State University Press, Columbus (1971)

Wilpert, Joseph, *Roma Sotteranea*, Rome (1903)

Wilpert, Joseph, *Die Römisch Mosaiken und Malereien ...* , vols. III & IV, Freiburg (1916)

Wilson, Elaine, *The Lost Dove*, Element Books, Shaftesbury (1998)

Wind, Edgar, *Pagan Mysteries in the Renaissance*, Faber & Faber, London (1958)

Woodcock, Thomas & Robinson, John Martin, *The Oxford Guide to Heraldry*, Oxford University Press, Oxford (1988)

Woodruff, Helen, *Illustrated Manuscripts of Prudentius*, Harvard University Press, Cambridge, Mass. (1930)

Woolley, Charles L., *The Sumerians*, Oxford University Press, Oxford (1928)

Wright, G.R.H, 'The Heritage of the Stylites', *Australian Journal of Biblical Archaeology*, vol. 1, no. 2 (1969)

Ziffer, Irit, *O my Dove, that art in the clefts of the rocks (The Dove Allegory in Antiquity)*, Eretz Museum, Tel Aviv (1998)

Index

Page numbers in **bold** refer to main sections devoted to the subject in question; those in *italic* refer to illustrations.